RESTLESS GENIUS
The Story of Virginia Woolf

RESTLESS GENIUS
The Story of Virginia Woolf

Virginia Brackett

MORGAN
REYNOLDS
Publishing, Inc.

620 South Elm Street, Suite 223
Greensboro, North Carolina 27406
http://www.morganreynolds.com

RESTLESS GENIUS: THE STORY OF VIRGINIA WOOLF

Copyright © 2004 by Virginia Brackett

Library of Congress Cataloging-in-Publication Data

Brackett, Virginia.
  Restless genius : the story of Virginia Woolf / Virginia Brackett.
    p. cm. — (World writers)
  Includes bibliographical references and index.
  ISBN 1-931798-37-0 (Lib. bdg.)
    1. Woolf, Virginia, 1882-1941—Juvenile literature. 2. Novelists,
English—20th century—Biography—Juvenile literature. [1. Woolf,
Virginia, 1882-1941. 2. Authors, English. 3. Women—Biography.] I.
Title. II. Series.
  PR6045.O72Z54357 2004
  823'.912—dc22

                            2003025043

Printed in the United States of America
First Edition

Sandra Cisneros

Virginia Woolf

Edgar Allan Poe

Jane Addams

Isak Dinesen

H.P. Lovecraft

Gwendolyn Brooks

Richard Wright

Henry Wadsworth Longfellow

Nathaniel Hawthorne

Stephen Crane

F. Scott Fitzgerald

Langston Hughes

Washington Irving

Edgar Rice Burroughs

H.G. Wells

Sir Arthur Conan Doyle

Isaac Asimov

Bram Stoker

Mary Shelley

Jules Verne

Ida Tarbell

George Orwell

Mary Wollstonecraft

World
Writers

To Lisa, who gave me the diaries

Contents

Virginia Woolf (1882-1941)
(Photograph by Lenare.)

Chapter One

Adeline Virginia Stephen

On a brisk October day in 1928, Virginia Woolf addressed an audience of young students at Girton College, a woman's school in Cambridge, England. Woolf did not make many public appearances, but she had accepted invitations to lecture twice in the same month at two different women's colleges. The topic of her talk was "Women and Fiction," which reflected her long held concern about the place of women in the history of writing.

Virginia had been educated mostly at home, as had many young women of the late nineteenth century in Great Britain. As the Victorian era drew to a close, women's roles were changing. No more, she told her audience, would they be expected to serve only as "looking-glasses possessing the magic and delicious power of reflecting the figure of man at twice its natural size." After her lecture, Virginia mused in her diary, "I fancy sometimes the world changes."

Woolf used her lecture to encourage women to take charge of their creativity and to demand a place in the writing world. She pointed out that few nonfiction works about women or works of fiction with strong women characters were actually written by women. How strange, she said, that men should presume to know more about how women thought and felt than did women themselves. Not only that, many male authors wrote with the assumption that women were inferior. Woolf had studied numerous such volumes, and mentioned one in particular written by a professor she refused to name. As she read it, she said, "My cheeks had burned. I had flushed with anger."

Woolf challenged her audience to correct the shortage of women writers. She cautioned that young women who wanted to write would have to defeat many stereotypes. They would have to struggle to be treated as individuals apart from the roles they filled in their homes and families. In order to live a life of the mind and make dreams into reality, women writers needed a place where they could dedicate themselves to thinking, writing, and creating, a place Woolf referred to as a room of their own. Woolf's certainty that her audience could achieve the goals she put before them reflected how much her own confidence had grown over the years. There was a time, however, when she had not been so self-assured.

A year later, Woolf published a book entitled *A Room of One's Own* that drew from these autumn talks. The book was later called "the first major achievement of feminist criticism in the English language." The analogy

Virginia's mother and father, Julia and Leslie Stephen, shared interests in literature, politics, and other issues. *(The Royal Photographic Society and the National Portrait Gallery, London.)*

of having a room of one's own reflected Woolf's belief that women deserved to be their own people, not defined only as wives, mothers, sisters, and daughters.

Adeline Virginia Stephen seemed destined to become a writer. She was born in 1882 to talented and accomplished literary parents. Her large family had a tremendous influence on her, eventually defining both her lack of self-confidence and her artistic ability. Her father, Leslie Stephen, edited the well-known *Dictionary of National Biography* and was one of England's most celebrated men of letters. Her mother, Julia Prinsep Jackson Duckworth Stephen, wrote tracts about the charity work with which she was nearly always busy. A celebrated beauty, Julia Stephen had served as the model for a famous painting of the Virgin Mary, *The Annunciation,* by Edward Burne-Jones. Virginia matured in a rare environment of culture and creativity headed by famous—and demanding—parents.

Both of Virginia's parents had been married before, and both were from distinguished families. Leslie Stephen's grandfather, William Wilberforce, was an early advocate for the eradication of slavery. Leslie's deeply religious father, James Stephen, campaigned against slavery too, and he dedicated much of his life to helping others. He also earned a knighthood from Queen Victoria. Leslie's mother, Jane, lived a life dedicated to public service. Her humorous manner helped to balance her husband's more somber demeanor. Family members said that Virginia Stephen had inherited her creative talent from her great-grandfather, her sense of humor from her grandmother, and her depressive tendencies from her grandfather.

Leslie Stephen attended Cambridge University and in 1859 he dedicated his life to the Anglican Church. He soon developed doubts about organized religion, however, and left the faith to become an intellectual and a writer.

In 1867, Leslie married Minnie Thackeray, daughter of the author William Makepeace Thackeray. They had one daughter, Laura, who was developmentally disabled. Leslie began editing the *Cornhill Magazine* in 1871. Their marriage was happy, but Minnie died suddenly during her second pregnancy, on Leslie's forty-second birthday in 1875. As Leslie grieved for his wife, the recently widowed Julia Duckworth, a friend of Minnie's, came to comfort him.

Julia's father had been a doctor in Calcutta, India, where Julia and her two sisters were born. Julia took the Victorian ideal of serving others to heart. One of her friends had written a series of poems titled *The Angel in the House* that praised women who could manage large families, serve others, and remain pure and angelic. Julia did her utmost to live up to this standard.

An often-photographed beauty, Julia had rejected many suitors before settling on a handsome, wealthy lawyer named Herbert Duckworth. Happily married, they had a son, George, and a daughter, Stella. In 1870, while Julia was pregnant with their third child, Herbert died. Gerald was born six weeks later. Disillusioned and unhappy following her husband's death, Julia rejected the religion of her youth. Like many other intellectuals in late Victorian England, she turned away from the explanations about the world offered by religion, embracing instead new scientific theories, particularly the theory of natural selection put forth in Charles Darwin's *Origin of Species.*

After her husband's death, Julia read a book Leslie Stephen had written titled *Essays on Freethinking and Plainspeaking.* Comforted by the author's suggestion that one did not need traditional religion in order to find meaning in life, Julia began to ease her grief by performing good works. In 1876, she helped Leslie, Laura, and Leslie's sister-in-law move into the house next door to her own. The two single parents developed a close relationship, and the following year Leslie proposed to Julia.

The Stephen family lived for many years in this house at 22 Hyde Park Gate.

Julia doubted that she was intelligent enough to marry such a well-educated man. Leslie Stephen's *History of English Thought in the Eighteenth Century* was a highly respected work. Leslie refused to be deterred, however, and the two married on March 26, 1878.

Julia and Leslie Stephen established a busy household with their four children at 22 Hyde Park Gate, in the heart of London. Leslie's daughter Laura was seven, and Julia's two sons, George and Gerald, were ten and seven. Her daughter Stella was eight. Julia, who was thirty-two when she married Stephen, delivered four more babies between 1879 and 1883: Vanessa, Thoby, Virginia, and Adrian. Eventually the dark Victorian house was expanded from five to seven stories to make room for the eight children and the servants who cared for them.

Famous artists and writers often visited the Stephen home. The Boston poet James Russell Lowell (of the legendary family that also included the later poets Amy and Robert Lowell), Leslie's former father-in-law W. M. Thackeray, British writers Thomas Hardy and George Meredith, and the great American expatriate novelist Henry James were frequent guests. Literature at this time was going through great shifts, and some of the most exciting changes were related to the structure of the novel. Thackeray's novels were bitterly funny satires about self-centered Victorians. Meredith, too, combined humor and intellect, while Hardy used his interest in science to produce naturalistic novels of everyday life full of tragedy and frustration. Henry James took the novel in a new direction when he moved on from his early realistic works to novels and stories that dived deeply into the psychology of his characters. These works innovatively allowed emotional changes, rather than action, to propel the narrative.

Henry James became the Stephen children's favorite visitor. They would watch as he leaned his chair back on two legs during intense conversations and hoped he might topple over. One day he finally did, and the children rolled on the floor with laughter as James picked himself up without interrupting his conversation.

Vanessa, the first baby of the new family, was a favorite of Leslie's daughter, Stella. Stella celebrated her tenth birthday on May 30, 1879, the day Vanessa was born, and thought of the baby as a birthday present. Stella, nicknamed "Bunch" by her father, became a surrogate mother to Vanessa, as well as to Thoby, who was born a year later. Vanessa impressed her father with her nurturing spirit and her love for Thoby. The siblings benefited from their close relationship when their mother left the family for a time in 1881 to care for her ill sister. This was the first of several long absences for Julia, who was so devoted to caring for others that she would sometimes be away from her own family for weeks or even months at a time.

Although Julia and Leslie had not planned to have more children, Virginia was born on January 25, 1882. James Russell Lowell accepted an invitation to be a sort of godparent to her. Julia was too weak to care for the other children after Virginia's birth, so Vanessa, Thoby, Stella, and Gerald stayed for a time with their grandparents.

Meanwhile, Leslie began work on a new project, editing an enormous biographical dictionary of English historical figures. The book became one of the century's most important reference works. Soon after Virginia was born, Leslie declared that he and Julia were finished having children. Julia was likely already pregnant with her last child, though, when Leslie made his statement.

Because Julia's final pregnancy came so soon after Virginia's birth, Virginia was weaned more quickly than was usual. She viewed the separation as a rejection by her mother, whose attention she craved, and she reacted by fighting with the next oldest child, Thoby. The family expected that Virginia and the new baby, Adrian, would become as close as Vanessa and Thoby were, but Virginia always preferred her older siblings.

One incident during Virginia's childhood might have

Virginia (left) and Vanessa Stephen playing cricket at Talland House, the family's summer retreat on the southern coast of England, in 1894. The sisters would have a close relationship throughout their lives. *(Photograph from the collection of Quentin Bell.)*

contributed to her later emotional problems. When she was four, she later wrote, her half brother Gerald Duckworth "explored" her body and touched her "private parts." Some have wondered if Virginia's being uncomfortable about sex as an adult was perhaps triggered by this negative experience in her childhood.

The four youngest Stephen children lived in two nurseries on the house's top level. Adrian, who turned out to be Julia's favorite child, stayed aloof from the other three, who formed a strong supportive group that retained its strength into adulthood. In contrast to Vanessa, a "serene and practical" girl, Virginia could be "wild and impish" and her mood was changeable. Sometimes she refused to speak at all; other times, she expressed her opinion too freely.

On the surface, Julia Stephen seemed to be the perfect Victorian wife and mother, dedicated to the lives of others. But she was also ambitious and used her nursing experience as the basis for an intelligent and practical book titled *Notes for Sick Rooms*. Although she supported a woman's right to work outside the home, she did not think women should challenge established societal roles. In 1889, Julia joined the writers Octavia Hill and Mrs. Humphry Ward in signing an "Appeal Against Female Suffrage," that was published in the journal *Nineteenth Century*.

Julia devoted a great deal of her energy to service work; the rest of it went to her family. Leslie could be cheerful and energetic with the younger children, but he was often highly critical and demanding of Julia and

Stella. He also suffered several emotional breakdowns.

Both Julia and Leslie tutored Virginia in reading, but her education was often interrupted by visitors and the Stephen family's frequent trips. The family was traveling in the Swiss Alps on Virginia's seventh birthday. Leslie was gone for her ninth, but wrote a letter home praising Virginia's writing ability and predicting that she would have a successful career as a writer. Others in the family also noticed Virginia's talent. Her grandmother thought one letter the young girl had written was so lovely, she wanted to frame it. Virginia often entertained the family and their guests with her lively tales.

During summer vacations the Stephens moved to their second home, Talland House. The children loved the house, which overlooked the fishing village of St. Ives, in Cornwall, England. From there they sailed to a local lighthouse with their father, who also spent hours hiking with them along the coast. These outings nourished Virginia's keen imagination.

Back in London, famous painters were among the regular visitors to the Stephen home, and they contributed to the artistic environment. Vanessa, surely influenced by her nurturing surroundings, developed a talent for painting at an early age. The two sisters' artistic natures drew them together, but their competitive attitudes sometimes led to arguments. One ongoing disagreement was over which of the arts, writing or painting, was the most pure.

In 1891, Julia left for a time to care for her mother. During her absence, Virginia grew closer to her father.

Although both he and Virginia were "hardworking, ambitious, intense, hypersensitive, obsessively literary and brilliant," Virginia would become the genius her father only dreamed of becoming. Unfortunately, she also inherited his tendency toward depression and his quick temper. Leslie spoke of Virginia as his spirited daughter, but her mother considered her mischievous. Virginia was closest to her father, but wished she could be as close to her mother. When Julia's mother became so ill that she had to move into the Stephen household, Virginia had yet another person to compete with for her mother's attention.

At age nine, with Thoby's help, Virginia began her writing career when the two children started a weekly newspaper, the *Hyde Park Gate News.* The two "editors" confessed to playing tricks on their handicapped half sister and sending fake letters to their mother. Virginia never hesitated to declare her opinions in print, particularly about Adrian, whose relationship with Julia continued to make Virginia jealous. She described Adrian on his birthday as "nine in years" but "five in intellect." Virginia described her mother as having strict rules but being unfairly lenient with the boys. Sometimes Virginia could be coaxed into sharing her journal writing with visitors. Stella once recorded in her own diary that Henry James, George Meredith, Oliver Wendell Holmes, and James Russell Lowell found Virginia's journal entries delightful and encouraged her to continue writing.

In March of 1895, Virginia noted in the *Hyde Park Gate News* that her mother suffered from the flu, but later newspaper issues never mentioned her health. In April, Julia suffered from a sore throat as she cared for Virginia, who was sick with the flu. Virginia recovered, but Julia became weaker. She was bedridden, and her health continued to decline. When Virginia quietly left Julia's sickroom one day in early May, her mother spoke her last words to her. Using one of Virginia's nicknames, Julia said, "Hold yourself straight, my little Goat." Julia died on May 5, 1895. Her death devastated the family. Leslie Stephen would never recover.

Virginia did not realize how much her mother's death would affect her. She thought that, being used to her mother's long absences, she would easily adjust. In reality, the death of her mother left her emotionally numb. Thirteen-year-old Virginia's inability to deal with her grief led to her first severe depression, which eventually became a full-fledged mental breakdown. She would remember the scenes surrounding her mother's death for the rest of her life. She could describe the exact way Julia's doctor, Dr. Savage, looked when he said that "everything had come to an end," his head down and hands clasped behind his back.

Stella did her best to assume Julia's role of caring for the family, especially for Leslie. Although Leslie would not publish again for three years, he continued to study and write. In his grief, he became more critical than ever and difficult to be around. Stella tended to the household accounts, visited the ill and the poor, and saw her stepsister, Laura, each week in the institution where she had been sent to live. Virginia later wrote of Stella, "She grew whiter and whiter in her unbroken black dress."

Virginia was unable to write for two years after her mother's death. She did not record family events or her own feelings. Her pent up feelings of anger and guilt had a negative effect on her health. Like her father, she had a delicate mental and emotional balance. In October 1896, more than a year after Julia's death, Stella wrote a note about taking Virginia to the doctor, who said "she must do less lessons & be very careful not to excite herself—her pulse is 146. Father in a great state."

By 1897, Virginia was disobeying her doctor's orders to rest. She returned to her lessons and writing, and again began making frequent entries in her diary. Victorian-era rest treatments for women's health problems often included restrictions on physical and intellectual activity. Defying this notion, once Virginia began writing again, she also seemed to begin to heal. She worked on a piece titled "Eternal Miss Jan" that was likely autobiographical (the story no longer exists); "Miss Jan" was one of Virginia's many nicknames. She also began to walk with her father in Kensington Gardens and often accompanied him to the London Library, where he had succeeded Alfred Tennyson as president in 1892.

When Stella became engaged to Jack Hills in 1896, the family saw some hope for happiness. At one point, Virginia and Vanessa went with the couple on a vacation to the south coast of England. Virginia passed the time reading the Scottish poet and novelist Sir Walter Scott. She later claimed that watching Stella and Jack supplied her earliest vision of what she called "musical" love,

This photograph of Vanessa, Stella, and Virginia was taken a few months after their mother's death. *(Photograph from the collection of Quentin Bell.)*

even though she found the idea of romance frightening.

Leslie Stephen delayed Stella's marriage because he did not want her to abandon the family. Finally, on her own, Stella scheduled the ceremony for April 10, 1897. Virginia dreaded participating as a bridesmaid. Leslie tried to convince the newlyweds to live at 22 Hyde Park Gate, but Stella refused. She compromised by moving into nearby number 27 instead.

It now fell to Vanessa, as the oldest remaining daughter, to run the Stephen household, and she needed Virginia's help. However, Virginia had recently developed a fear of going into the busy London streets. Leslie grew impatient with her nervousness and felt she read too much, a surprising attitude coming from a man so immersed in the world of writing and literature. His irritation may have grown from his conviction, common at the time, that a woman's primary job was to care for her family. That attitude may have also contributed to the tone of one diary entry, in which he expressed frustration because Stella was sick. She was confined to bed, in her own house, unable to help the younger girls.

When Stella moved out, Vanessa and Virginia rear-ranged the children's rooms. They no longer shared a room, and a former nursery became Vanessa's art studio. Virginia grew lonely in her own room. Leslie remained distracted and distant, and Vanessa kept busy with her art and household duties. Once Stella became ill, Virginia tired of having to visit yet another sickroom. She later understood that her anger was really jealousy over the attention Stella received.

In July 1897, doctors decided to operate on Stella. She seemed to come through the surgery well, but died less than twenty-four hours later. She likely died from perito-nitis, a bacterial infection of the abdominal region. She may also have been pregnant.

Virginia was fifteen when Stella died, and wrote that she could hardly express her grief. The next month, though, she began to study at King's College in the University of London. All of the Stephens were busy. Adrian had begun attending day school. In 1899, Thoby enrolled at Trinity College, Cambridge; Adrian would later follow him there.

At Cambridge, Thoby joined a group of five first-year students who called themselves the Midnight Society, later nicknaming themselves the Apostles. They earned their name because every Saturday at midnight they would meet in one of their rooms to read poetry.

Meanwhile, Vanessa was at the age when she was supposed to look for a husband. Although she was reluctant to do so, she attended a round of coming-out parties, the traditional formal introduction to society that was expected of young women from the upper middle class. Virginia was disturbed when Vanessa attached her-

Thoby Stephen enrolled at Trinity College, Cambridge, in 1899. *(Photograph from the collection of Quentin Bell.)*

self to Jack Hills, who had sought the comfort of the Stephen family following Stella's death. As the relationship threatened to become a romance, Virginia's concern grew. English law made it illegal for a man to marry his sister-in-law, and the family feared a scandal.

Virginia was further upset because she felt Leslie was often verbally abusive to Vanessa. To make up for their father's lack of support, Virginia encouraged her sister's painting. In 1901, Vanessa was admitted to the highly competitive Royal Academy to study art. There, she studied with the famous painter John Singer Sargent and won highest honors in a school competition.

After her mother's death, Virginia had to learn how to cope with her father's moodiness and depression. *(Photograph from the collection of Quentin Bell.)*

At King's College, Virginia loved the student's life. An excellent student of Greek and Latin, Virginia thought all young women should study classical languages. She began to develop her own ideas about art. She thought art should imitate life, but wondered if it could do more than that. Before long, she decided to devote her life to exploring the inner life of her characters, hoping to reveal a deeper, more profound level of truth than was usually found in realistic fiction.

By the 1900s, Leslie Stephen had disappeared into a morose shell. He was often sick and had become increasingly deaf, which added to his moodiness. He received a knighthood in 1902 for his literary achievements, but even this high honor did not wake him from his depression. He badgered Vanessa and demanded Virginia's company. She read to him and endured his complaints that his daughters would land them all in the poorhouse.

Virginia performed well in her language studies, but she decided not to complete a degree at King's College. Instead, she stayed home to work at perfecting her writing style. Vanessa began traveling to study art, going first of all to France. Thoby, meanwhile, spent most of his time at school. To help relieve her loneliness, Virginia developed friendships with several women, including her cousin Madge Symonds Vaughan, whose father was the writer John Addington Symonds. She wrote many letters to Madge and to another friend, Violet Dickinson.

Although she was considered attractive, Virginia remained baffled by the relationships between men and women. Still, like other girls their age, she and Vanessa attended spring and summer dances. In 1901, Virginia and Vanessa traveled with a chaperone to Cambridge to visit their brother Thoby. The sisters were finally able to meet the Midnight Society they had heard so much about. The other four members of the group were Clive Bell, Lytton Strachey, Saxon Sydney-Turner, and Leonard Woolf. Virginia did not seem particularly impressed by any of the young men, but they would eventually become a vital part of her life.

Chapter Two

The Bloomsbury Group

After his first meeting with Virginia and Vanessa Stephen, Leonard Woolf compared them to two spirited horses: they appeared calm on the surface but carried a warning "at the back of the eye." He was impressed by their "great intelligence, hypercritical, sarcastic, satirical." But it was their beauty that "literally took one's breath away." Although Virginia and Vanessa had officially entered society, neither enjoyed formal parties or boring chatter. They had no desire to emulate their mother.

The intellectual conversation of the Apostles was what they craved. Thoby described Lytton Strachey as a genius and a wit, Clive Bell as a poet and even better horseman, and Saxon Sydney-Turner as a logical atheist. Leonard Woolf was less easily defined than the others, although he was clearly very intelligent. Eventually the group added more members and became famous as the Bloomsbury Group. They attracted worldwide attention for their bohemian lifestyle and intellectual and artistic

pursuits, and the word "Bloomsbury" soon became syn-
onymous with a modern, elitist outlook. It was through
the Bloomsbury Group that Virginia discovered what
would become the core of her aesthetic vision.
The intellectual conversation that Virginia so valued
occurred less and less frequently at home. Leslie received few guests and the family followed the same
routine everyday. Vanessa began most mornings by riding
her horse up and down a nearby stretch of road then
joined her brother Gerald for breakfast at 8:30. Leslie
and Adrian took breakfast next, with Adrian generally
late for school and missing part of his supplies. Leslie
often bemoaned the lack of mail, repeating a favorite
phrase, "Everyone has forgotten me," or complaining
"we shall be ruined" when reviewing bills. Vanessa met
with the cook in the basement to plan the family meals,
then left for art school. George and Virginia breakfasted
last, with George likely telling Virginia all about his
social triumphs of the previous evening, then departing
for his unpaid secretarial position. Leslie isolated himself in his study for the rest of the morning while Virginia
moved upstairs to the old nursery, now her office. There
she read Sir Walter Scott, or Sophocles or Euripides in
the original Greek, and sometimes visited with friends.
She also wrote, standing at her high desk. She liked to
stand while writing because it allowed her to feel kinship
with Vanessa, who stood at her easel to paint.

Virginia and Vanessa still argued over whether painting or writing was the purest art. They combined their
interests, though, to develop skill in the craft of book-

binding. Virginia's fascination with books, and Vanessa's with the various materials involved in their construction, made the sisters perfect partners for such work.

When Vanessa would go away on tours to study and view art, Virginia became lonely. In one letter, she complained that Vanessa received all of the attention and had the most friends. She feared that she might lose Vanessa, either to her painting or to other friends. While she still talked with her father, his increasing surliness alienated Virginia, as it did most of the family. Virginia longed for the company of the Apostles.

Virginia found some refuge in the unwavering friendship of Violet Dickinson. She corresponded often with Violet, giving herself nicknames in the letters and portraying herself as a shy animal in need of petting and cuddling. Virginia felt comfortable with Violet in a way that she could not in London's high society. She discussed her failure as a socialite in one letter: "I think Providence inscrutably decreed some other destiny for me." This feeling of isolation, of not being quite part of the world around her, would later be a common trait in the characters in her novels.

After years of caring for her moody father, Virginia came to resent his ill health. She suspected him of faking his ailments, saying she wished she could do the same and have women waiting on and caring for her, too. When visitors came to the house, they had to shout into Leslie's ear trumpet, but they could easily hear his protests and insults. Leslie's condition worsened and in December 1902 he had surgery for intestinal cancer. In early 1903, doctors gave him only six months to live.

Despite this gloomy atmosphere, Virginia continued her journal entries. She wrote an essay titled "The Serpentine," based on the factual account of a woman who drowned herself in the man-made Serpentine Lake that crossed Hyde Park and Kensington Gardens. Virginia fixated on the woman's suicide note, and on how lonely she must have been. While fascinated by such human drama, she continued to wonder about the mission of art. In another essay, titled "Country Reading," she questioned whether art could possibly reproduce life as people perceived it or if it should even attempt to do so. It was an important argument, one that Vanessa also struggled with in her painting. Vanessa had begun to experiment with methods used in impressionism, a technique introduced by French painters. Impressionist artists typically used fragmented strokes of pure color to convey fleeting impressions of scenes or objects. They also incorporated the changing effects of light, arguing that because an object's appearance was altered by the shifting patterns of light, no one true image could ever totally represent it. Impressionists thought that paintings that tried to be realistic could never succeed in capturing the transitory nature of the world.

Virginia wondered whether impressionist techniques might be applicable to fiction writing. While her father had been an early influence, the artistic ideas of his generation did not apply to what she wanted to do with her work. She envisioned a plot that did not move in a straight line, one that abandoned traditional storytelling devices such as beginnings, middles, and ends, as well as the typical dramatic climax. Not every narrative, she believed, had to be told in the same way.

As Leslie's health worsened, his visitors exhausted Virginia. She longed for a regular routine. In 1903, he celebrated a final Christmas with his family. Though he was in good spirits, he felt too weak to recite, as he had every year, John Milton's "Ode on the Nativity." He died on February 22, 1904.

Seeking some relief from their sorrow, the family traveled to the English coast. There, at Pemberton, Virginia had the beginning of an idea for her first novel. She later wrote that she had known since age sixteen that she would write a novel, but only at age twenty-one, while walking along the water's edge, could she see her vision clearly. Although the plot was still only loosely defined, she knew that she would incorporate a new approach to storytelling in this novel. Like a ship hidden by the ocean fog, the structure was not yet fully discernible, but it was there. It simply had to emerge and take shape.

The writing, however, did not initally proceed well. Virginia missed her father and felt she had not told him often enough how much she loved him. She became increasingly agitated and Vanessa feared she might have a breakdown. Virginia was worried as well. She wrote later that she kept trying to prove nothing was wrong although she suspected something was. The same sharp, creative mind that was struggling to revolutionize writing was also threatened by the outside world.

Vanessa, Thoby, and Virginia planned a trip to Italy

where they would join Violet Dickinson in Florence. They hoped travel might soothe Virginia's anxiety. Things went well until Virginia became disenchanted with Italy. She seemed to be irritated by Vanessa's pleasure at viewing great works of art by the Italian Renaissance masters Tintoretto, Titian, Sando Botticelli, and Filippo Lippi. Virginia wanted to share Vanessa's enthusiasm, but she began to feel closed in. Even Violet could not calm her. Virginia wrote that Venice made her feel like a caged bird. That image came to symbolize the plight of women in the Victorian age: beautiful, decorative creatures trapped in golden prisons. The vision of the unwritten novel that had so thrilled Virginia a few months earlier now seemed lost, held captive by a thickening fog.

In April, Vanessa, Virginia, and Thoby spent time in Paris. There they visited the studio of Auguste Rodin, famous for his sculpture *The Thinker,* among many others, and considered by many the most important sculptor of his time. They also met up with Thoby's friends, including Clive Bell, who took an interest in Vanessa. Vanessa seemed to blossom during the trip, awash in attention from Bell and feeling somewhat liberated since her father's death. Her enthusiasm dismayed Virginia, who suffered headaches and fatigue.

Back in England by May, Virginia was desperate to get to work, but was too exhausted and emotional to focus. The strain of dealing with guilt and sorrow at the loss of her mother, then Stella, and finally her father, had left her feeling helpless and overwhelmed. She began to have hallucinations. She imagined that birds outside her window sang in Greek, and that King Edward VII hid in the azalea bushes, cursing. She stayed for a time with Violet, who tried to comfort her. Restless and agitated, Virginia threw herself out a window. The fall did not result in injury, as the window was close to the ground, but this would not be the last time she tried to hurt herself. For the remainder of the summer of 1904, Virginia experienced a terrifying madness.

Through September, Virginia gathered her strength and tried to return to her writing. The rest of the family had moved on after Leslie's death. Adrian had begun his studies at Cambridge, and Vanessa and Thoby supervised a move from Hyde Park to Gordon Square, a section of London just three blocks from the British Museum. Not as fashionable as Hyde Park, Gordon Square allowed the Stephens to live comfortably on their inheritance. Their half brothers had their own lives. Gerald Duckworth lived alone, and after George Duckworth married Lady Margaret Herbert in the fall of 1904 the couple moved into an elegant house of their own.

Thoby occupied himself with collecting material about his father for a biography slated to be written by Frederic Maitland. Vanessa decorated the house and made it clear she wanted no aunts or other relatives moving in. Virginia's doctor felt that London would not be good for her, so she went to live with her aunt in Cambridge. She felt jealous of Vanessa's freedom and resentful at being kept away from the new house.

When Maitland asked Virginia to help him write her father's biography, she jumped at the opportunity. Her enthusiasm diminished when she discovered he only wanted her to copy selections from Leslie's papers. Virginia wanted to write part of the biography herself. Eventually, Maitland recognized her talent and asked her to write her own additions to the biography. Virginia made a short visit to London in October, but immediately felt ill again. Vanessa insisted she return to Cambridge for continued rest and treatment. Vanessa wrote to Virginia that she should stay away from London for her own benefit, not because she was not wanted. Virginia did not believe her sister, and they entered a period in their relationship that was haunted by jealousy and paranoia.

Vanessa invited Virginia to London again in November on the condition that she return to Cambridge for a stay with their cousins, Madge and Will Vaughan. On November 17, while Virginia was in London, Leonard Woolf came to dinner. Although an intelligent and informed man, he did not score well on university exams and could not remain a student at Cambridge. Instead, he took a position in public service. Woolf planned to become a colonial administrator in Ceylon—present-day Sri Lanka. After the dinner, just before his twenty-fourth birthday, he gathered some books and his fox terrier and left England. Virginia would not see him again for years, but she clearly made an impression on him that evening, as he began discussing her in his correspondence with other members of their circle.

Virginia was still busy working on her father's biography. She had Vanessa review the letters written by their parents that she wanted to include in the book. Vanessa considered the letters too private for public eyes and only reluctantly gave in to her sister's wishes. Virginia saw Vanessa's attitude as more evidence of the widening gap between them. In one way, the distance helped Virginia's writing. She began writing to gain the public's approval, rather than that of her sister.

Virginia had the support of Violet Dickinson, who had taken some of Virginia's writing to the editor of a well-known periodical, *The Guardian.* He was intrigued and asked to see more. Although he did not accept everything Virginia sent him, he did purchase two of her book reviews to print. When another periodical rejected Virginia's work, she took the rejection bravely. Violet's encouragement had led to Virginia's being published for the first time and now she wanted to publish more, even if she had to suffer rejection first.

When Virginia at last moved back to London, in January 1905, the bond between the sisters again grew stronger. Free of adult supervision, they began to enjoy themselves. There was no need to dress up for dinner or to go out into society. Instead, they could make friends with people of their choosing, people interested in social reform, philosophical topics, and the future of art.

In February, Thoby, who was studying to become an attorney, took a break to visit with friends in Bloomsbury. This first gathering, on February 16, which included only Thoby, Vanessa, Virginia and Saxon Sydney-Turner, was the birth of the Bloomsbury Group. Clive Bell, Lytton Strachey, and Desmond MacCarthy soon became regular fixtures at the Stephen home. Virginia was initially frightened by the outspoken Lytton Strachey, but she soon learned that he could be a compassionate and wise friend. The group sometimes stayed up talking until two or three in the morning. Virginia wrote of being "filled with wonder" after dropping out of an argument the oth-

Clive Bell and Thoby Stephen became close friends in the Bloomsbury Group. *(Photograph from the collection of Angelica Garnett.)*

ers were building and then listening as they continued, "piling stone upon stone . . . long after it had completely soared above my sight." She felt that she glimpsed "something miraculous happening high up in the air."

The Bloomsbury Group became controversial in some quarters for their rejection of Victorian ideals in favor of new, modern principles. Not only did no one dress up for Bloomsbury gatherings, Virginia and Vanessa were treated as part of the group, not just as gracious hostesses. The purpose of the meetings was not to find a husband, but to exchange ideas. The two women thrived in this setting, but a disapproving Henry James wondered how they could have chosen such acquaintances.

Clive Bell, who had become Thoby's closest friend, had a reputation as a playboy who enjoyed hunting and other outdoor pleasures. His interest in art, along with his appreciation for beautiful women, drew him to Vanessa, but she rejected his marriage proposal in 1905. Another young artist, Duncan Grant, joined the group that same year. Handsome, talented, and charming, he had love affairs with several of the men in the group, including Adrian Stephen. He also took an interest in Vanessa.

Virginia, meanwhile, proclaimed herself well at last, and filled pages in her diary. An editor from the *Times Literary Supplement* asked her to contribute book reviews to the respected magazine. During the Bloomsbury Group meetings, she absorbed what the Cambridge-educated men had to say then hurried off to read about the topics. When she and Vanessa added their own opinions to the discussions, they were delighted to find that "the young men . . . criticized our arguments as severely as their own."

In April of 1905, Virginia and Adrian visited Spain for a week, a journey that influenced her first novel. Initially called *Melymbrosia,* it was eventually published as *The Voyage Out.* Upon returning to London, Virginia found that one of her book reviews had been rejected because, in the editor's opinion, it did not represent serious criticism. Her writing was strong enough, however, that the same editor asked her to review three books on Spain.

A trip later in the year to Talland House brought back

many memories. While sailing, Virginia noted an image that she would repeatedly write about in the future—a dark fin rising above the water's surface. She was intrigued that the fin could either be that of a dolphin, signaling safety, or a shark, signaling danger. Virginia was fascinated that these two possibilities were both suggested by the same image. She decided to remain at Talland House through October and Vanessa returned to London. Vanessa had become part of the Friday Club, a fine-arts discussion group, where she was joined by Clive Bell.

Virginia soon took another step toward independence. She accepted an invitation to teach classes at Morley College for women. It was an opportunity for Virginia to meet and develop relationships with women from the lower economic classes that London society considered to be her inferiors. For the first time, she met people who lived in the Grub Street area, one of London's poorest quarters. She taught at Morley College through 1907, lecturing mainly on history. As she grew closer to her students, she urged them to write, believing it was one way they could help improve their situations.

In the late fall of 1906, Adrian, Thoby, Vanessa, Virginia, and Violet decided to take a long trip to Greece. As they traveled, Virginia tried to write her impressions of what she saw but found herself frustrated by the limitations of language. She had so many thoughts and emotions that she could not express with words. She began to wonder if visual arts such as painting might indeed be more effective at conveying the artist's meaning.

Talland House, the Stephen family home on the southern coast of England, provided Virginia with many of the images she used in her fiction. *(Photograph by Ann James.)*

Vanessa became sick on the trip. By the time they returned to London, Thoby and Violet were also ill with malaria. Adrian and Virginia had to care for their sister and brother "in the midst of nurses, bedpans, carbolic and doctors." Vanessa slowly recovered but Thoby did not respond to the treatment. After several days, a nurse realized that Thoby's high fever was a symptom of typhoid and that Violet Dickinson had the same disease.

Thoby seemed to recover briefly, but on November 20, 1906, he died. His death sent the Stephen family and the Bloomsbury Group into shock. The Stephens had to deal with the loss of yet another family member. Virginia maintained her composure for the sake of Violet, who was judged by her doctor to be too weak to learn the news. For several weeks, in her letters to Violet, Virginia continued to write about Thoby as though he were still alive. Maintaining this fiction was extremely difficult.

Thoby's death changed the family dynamic yet again. He had always been particularly close to Vanessa, who missed him even more than Virginia did. Two days after Thoby's death, Vanessa accepted a proposal of marriage from the persistent Clive Bell. Virginia was dismayed by her decision—she felt abandoned. Though it was Vanessa he married, Clive Bell also had a deep appreciation for Virginia, especially for her talent as a writer. Clive and Virginia maintained a prolific correspondence, and it was he who encouraged her early writing. Clive's affection for Virginia was romantic, as well; though she refused his advances, Clive flirted with her regularly.

When Vanessa and Clive married, he moved into the

house at 46 Gordon Square. Virginia and her brother Adrian moved into a new house at 29 Fitzroy Square. The two had never been close, and sharing a house brought out the worst in their relationship. She wrote, "We were the most incompatible of people. . . . We drove each other perpetually into frenzies of irritation or into the depths of gloom." To make matters worse, the meetings of the Bloomsbury Group began to trail off. With Thoby gone and Vanessa married to Clive, the group dynamics shifted and became strained. Virginia wrote that the meetings often failed, and afterward, "Adrian stalked off to his room, I to mine, in complete silence."

Fortunately, for the first time in her life, these outside events did not affect Virginia's health. Instead, she continued work on *Melymbrosia,* the novel she had been thinking about for years. Her contact with Violet became more infrequent and she became closer to Madge Symonds, the cousin-by-marriage with whom she had stayed following her previous breakdown.

The next months not only challenged Virginia's creativity, but her sexual identity as well. Clive continued to flirt with Virginia. She and Vanessa were also the only female members of the Bloomsbury Group, and the male members often had frank discussions about sex and sexuality in their presence. Several core members of the Bloomsbury Group were homosexual, and intimate same-sex relationships were common.

In late 1907, Vanessa annouced she was pregnant. Virginia again felt betrayed and left out. Clive made matters worse by neglecting his pregnant wife to pay

Virginia and Clive Bell, on the beach at Dorset, 1910. *(Photograph from the collection of Angelica Garnett.)*

more attention to her sister. Virginia showed him her early work on her novel, and after one reading, he wrote that her words revealed "in a person I cared for, genius."

His encouragement was exactly what Virginia needed to keep writing, and his flattery reassured her during an otherwise difficult period. The letters the two exchanged became more and more intimate.

Feeling confused by Clive's attention, Virginia knew she needed something to help her focus on her writing. She hoped a change of scenery would do it and traveled again to Italy, where she continued to wrestle with her own philosophy of art. She hoped to "attain a different kind of beauty: achieve a symmetry by means of infinite discords, showing all the traces of the mind's passage through the world." She wanted to put together in writing the "shivering fragments" that represented the human thought process and create a beautiful whole. Clive had said she was approaching something new in her novel, but she did not share his confidence.

When Virginia returned to London, Clive continued his flirtation with her. Lytton Strachey was irritated by Clive's irresponsibility and selfishness. He knew that Virginia needed to write; it was critical to her sanity. Strachey decided to spend more time with Virginia. He accompanied her and Adrian on one of several trips she made back to Talland House. She hoped to revive her creativity through happy memories of her family.

When the Bells' first son, Julian, was born in 1908, Vanessa was entirely absorbed by motherhood. Clive complained that his wife no longer slept with him or had time to pay attention to him. Virginia listened to him but she was also very busy. The *Times Literary Supplement* published several of her reviews that year and *Cornhill,* the magazine her father had once edited, published eight of her essays. These essays about literature are considered to be some of the most perceptive of the time. Virginia continued work on her novel and managed to write and revise seven chapters. She also became involved in the campaign to get women the right to vote, although she had long claimed not to be interested in politics. In a moment of tenderness, Lytton Strachey proposed marriage and Virginia accepted, even though she knew he was homosexual. He broke the engagement a short time later. Strachey wrote to Leonard Woolf, still in Ceylon, about the engagement fiasco and suggested that Woolf propose to Virginia. In the meantime, Virginia rejected several other marriage proposals.

In 1909, Virginia received an inheritance from her aunt of £2,500. With this new financial freedom, she decided to go with the Bells on another trip to Italy. Vanessa felt threatened by the flirtation between Virginia and her husband, and the sisters' relationship was severely strained by the time they returned to London. Vanessa threw all of her energy into the exhibition of one of her paintings at the New English Art Club, and Clive distracted himself by rekindling an affair he had engaged in prior to his marriage. Virginia publicly praised Vanessa's art, but her sister remained distant, writing to Virginia that writers "do not know the joy of experimenting in a new medium" as visual artists do. Perhaps this was her way of disparaging her sister.

Vanessa and Clive's second son, Quentin Bell, was born in 1910. Whatever changing feelings Virginia had for her sister, she loved Vanessa's sons deeply.

Chapter Three

Mrs. Leonard Woolf

Early in 1910, Clive and Vanessa met Roger Fry, a forty-four-year-old former art buyer for the Metropolitan Museum in New York. Fry was a painter in his own right. Clive thought his work remarkable, and invited him to the Bloomsbury Group meetings. Fry spent much of his time and energy taking care of his mentally ill wife. Yet he was poised to lead a revolution in English art that would influence Vanessa and help show Virginia how she might revolutionize the art of writing.

Fry had begun to adopt the postimpressionist style, which up to that point had been used primarily by French painters. These artists did not concern themselves with presenting the world as it actually appeared but stressed instead the imitation of nature using only primary colors. Blended colors, such as green, which results from combining blue and yellow, were absent from their work. They also analyzed how light affected objects. The postimpressionist painters Paul Cézanne and Vincent

Van Gogh applied their colors onto the canvas in vivid strokes. Geometric forms, such as triangles and squares, often centered the images. This new style was shocking to those accustomed to traditional art, but Clive, Vanessa, and Virginia all found it fascinating.

An exhibit by the artists Fry supported appeared in London in November 1910. The public reacted violently

A self-portrait by Roger Fry. *(Musée d'Art Moderne, Paris.)*

to this postimpressionist exhibition, the first of its kind in London. They also reacted negatively to Fry. Although Vanessa became caught up in the new movement, Virginia was not initially as interested. But she could not ignore the commotion it produced. Soon everyone identified the Bloomsbury Group as supporters of postimpressionism.

In April of 1911, the Bells, a friend from Cambridge, and Roger Fry, traveled to Brussels, Belgium and then on to the ancient city of Constantinople to look at art. Clive went reluctantly, as Vanessa did not feel well, but his concern about leaving London seemed to have more to do with Virginia than with Vanessa's health. He feared his sister-in-law might fall in love with someone else while he was gone.

During the trip Vanessa fainted several times and finally collapsed. When Virginia learned of her sister's problems, she immediately left London to be with her. When she caught up with them, Virginia discovered that Fry had taken control of the situation and, Virginia believed, had rescued Vanessa from possible death. Virginia and Roger became close, but by the time the group returned to London she realized that Vanessa and Fry were in love, although both were married to others. Roger's wife lived in a mental institution, and Clive, already involved in an affair of his own, accepted Vanessa's romance with Fry. Virginia decided to accept the situation as well. Over time, the Bell marriage became a marriage between friends, not lovers. Clive and Vanessa would not divorce, but each would continue to have other relationships.

Virginia's new interest in postimpressionism and her growing emotional strength allowed her to become more involved than ever in the artistic debates of the Bloomsbury Group. She and Adrian decided to move to a new house they could share with friends. They found just the place at 38 Brunswick Square. Some of her family and acquaintances disapproved of the move because Virginia would share the house with three men. As for Virginia, she could not have been more pleased. John Maynard Keynes, who would become the most important economist of the twentieth century, shared the first floor with Duncan Grant; Adrian lived on the second;

Three central figures of the Bloomsbury Group, pictured in 1912. From left to right they are: Duncan Grant, John Maynard Keynes, and Clive Bell. *(Photograph from the collection of Quentin Bell.)*

Virginia on the third; and Leonard Woolf, who after more than six years in Ceylon was finally coming home, was going to move into rooms on the fourth floor.

Everything in Virginia's life was moving along except for her novel. Already into her sixth revision during a vacation to Talland in April 1911, she had finished only eight of the eventual twenty-seven chapters. By July, she had begun to suffer headaches and wrote to Vanessa, "I could not write, & all the devils came out—hairy black ones. To be 29 & unmarried—to be a failure—Childless—insane too, no writer." Another marriage proposal in November 1910 had not lifted her spirits. Leonard Woolf's arrival in June, however, stirred her interests.

Woolf had done a good job as an administrator, which surprised his friends. He resumed his friendships in the group that now included Walter Lamb, who would later become secretary of the prestigious Royal Academy, and the novelist E. M. Forster, who was called Morgan by the members. Leonard also rekindled his interest in Virginia Stephen.

One July evening in 1911, Leonard joined the Bells for dinner. Afterward, Virginia and Walter Lamb, whose proposal for marriage Virginia would later reject, dropped by. Virginia invited Leonard to visit her for a weekend in the country. He was unable to accept due to a prior engagement, but the two agreed to meet another time. Virginia went on her excursion with Lamb and the poet Rupert Brooke, and a short time later received a reminder from Leonard that she owed him a visit. In her return letter, she accepted the invitation and suggested

Asheham House, Virginia's country home in Sussex Downs in southern England, as painted by Vanessa in 1912.

they call each other by first names. A series of visits began.

That October, Virginia and Leonard were walking in the southern English countryside together when they discovered Asheham House, which would become the first of Virginia's country homes. She had originally asked Vanessa to share the lease, but Virginia and Leonard quickly took over the entire house. In December Woolf told Virginia that he loved her, and in January 1912 he proposed marriage. She asked for time to get to know him better, and he agreed to wait.

Vanessa enthusiastically supported Leonard's court-ship, writing to him, "You're the only person I know whom I can imagine as her husband." However, Virginia broke under the strain of the decision, underwent a mild nervous breakdown, and moved out of London to recuperate. From a nursing home in Twickenham, near London, she wrote Leonard notes making light of her situation. A less-devoted suitor might have been scared away by the breakdown, but Leonard was undeterred. Virginia spent most of her days working on her novel, a book that focuses on a young woman voyaging across the Atlantic, perhaps symbolizing Virginia's exploration of her own nature. The symbolism combines with the narrative to create a layered and unconventionally plotted novel.

As Leonard waited for Virginia, he also missed Ceylon and its people, who he had found fascinating. He started writing a novel about his experiences there titled *The Village in the Jungle*. He also considered returning to his post. But if he returned, he would be gone again for several years and would not be able to take Virginia with him. In February, he requested four months from his superiors to make up his mind. In April, he wrote to Virginia that he must marry her, saying "God, the happiness I've had by being with you & talking with you as I've sometimes felt it mind to mind together & soul to soul." She responded to the letter by regretting that he was ruining his career and explaining that she was "in a fog" through which she could not see, a fog much like the one that kept the rest of her novel hidden from her. She encouraged Leonard's affection, though, by acknowledging that when she was with him she had "some feeling which is permanent & growing." She also admitted that he had made her happy, and that was enough to convince Leonard to decide against the return to Ceylon.

Woolf resigned his position in May and by the end of the month, Virginia agreed to marry him. Family and friends later thought that her decision to marry Woolf probably saved her life and allowed her to develop as a writer. He provided her with the stability she needed to concentrate on her work.

In June, Virginia wrote about her upcoming wedding to Violet Dickinson: "I'm going to marry Leonard Woolf. He's a penniless Jew. I'm more happy than anyone ever said was possible—but I insist upon your liking him too." She had finally almost finished her novel and wrote "L. thinks my writing the best part of me." Violet did like Leonard, especially his support of Virginia's writing. Their wedding took place on August 10, 1912, and the couple settled down in Asheham House.

After the simple wedding, the newlyweds traveled to France, Spain, and Italy for a honeymoon. It was not a completely happy trip. Virginia had to try to come to terms with her attitude regarding sex. She had always disliked the idea of sex and now discovered that she also disliked the reality of it. She and Leonard spoke openly about the problem with Vanessa and others, but they could not resolve it. Vanessa believed that Virginia was unable to understand sexual passion. Virginia wanted a family but Leonard thought Virginia's mental health too precarious to raise children. He consulted with several doctors, including Dr. Savage, who waved away his concern and told him to have patience.

Back at Asheham House, Leonard and Virginia took advantage of the distance from their friends to focus on their work. Virginia read Leonard's novel and admired it. They were both happy when *The Village in the Jungle* was accepted for publication. It appeared in February 1913 to high critical acclaim and was reprinted twice more that year, remaining in print for several years to come. Critics proclaimed that no European novelist had succeeded in portraying "the mind and heart of the Far East" as well as Leonard Woolf had done.

Leonard worried about Virginia's health as she worked hard completing her novel, now titled *The Voyage Out*. Her half brother Gerald owned a publishing company and agreed to publish it. But as soon as it was accepted, Virginia slipped into a depression. She ended up once again at Twickenham, undergoing the traditional treatment of rest and a restricted diet. She stayed there for several weeks in July and August 1913. In her letters from Twickenham, she nicknamed Leonard "Mongoose." For herself she did not use her family nickname of "Goat." Instead, in one note she apologized for being an "appallingly stupid. . . mandril [sic]," referring to a large and brightly colored baboon. Choosing this nickname for herself reveals her continued lack of self-confidence.

When Virginia was discharged Leonard took her to Asheham but he feared she was suicidal. They returned to London and stayed with the Bells for a time. Virginia did not seem to be improving; both Vanessa and Clive expressed concern. When Leonard asked Dr. Savage whether Virginia should return to Twickenham, rather than go on a vacation as they had planned, the doctor urged Leonard to allow her to take a break from the institution. Toward the end of August, the Woolfs traveled to an inn they had always enjoyed, but Virginia became more agitated, argumentative, and delusional. She imagined that others laughed at her. She told Leonard that she was most terrified by the fact that she knew she was insane and would not be able to write again.

Back in London, they visited a specialist Leonard admired on September 9, 1913. The doctor told Virginia she must accept the fact that she was quite sick. When a second physician told her to return to Twickenham for further rest, Virginia was despondent.

The couple went to their previous address at Brunswick Square, and Vanessa came for a visit. Distracted by her own romantic problems, she had become less attentive to Virginia. Vanessa's relationship with Roger Fry had cooled and she was now in love with Duncan Grant. The only problem was that Duncan was in love with her brother, Adrian.

Being surrounded by the old Bloomsbury Group and her sister again made Virginia feel moody and exhausted. One afternoon while Leonard was out, she took a fatal dose of the sedative veronal. Discovering her unconcious when he returned, Leonard rushed her to have her stomach pumped. Had he not found her soon enough, Virgnina Woolf would have died. A few days later, government officials began an inquiry into her state of mind. They

Virginia and Leonard at Asheham House, 1913. *(Photograph from the collection of Angelica Garnett.)*

needed to decide whether she should be put in an asylum for her own safety. Once they were convinced her family could care for her, the commissioners decided not to interfere. Virginia's recovery proved slow, however, and publication of *The Voyage Out* had to be delayed.

George Duckworth provided the Woolfs with rooms in his large, elegant country house. Vanessa came to visit, but, suffering from depression herself, rarely stayed long. The Woolfs remained there for two months and nurses provided Virginia with around-the-clock care. The couple next moved back to Asheham for several months, accompanied by two nurses. The strain of Virginia's condition began to wear on Leonard, who left for a short time to visit Strachey. While away, he wrote to his wife daily, telling her how grateful he was that her suicide attempt had failed. Virginia improved slowly over the fall. They took occasional short trips around England, and in October 1914, they moved to Richmond.

Even while dealing with Virginia's care, Leonard had continued writing. His second novel, *The Wise Virgins,* was published in October 1914 to a dismal reception. It received negative reviews and sold poorly. The book was also highly autobiographical and made trouble between Leonard and his family. After reviewing an early draft, his mother had raised objections to much of the book. While Leonard revised some of the more controversial material, the final manuscript still contained unflattering characters based on his mother and sister. Later readers would find the book interesting primarily because of its characterizations of Harry, a Jewish painter, and Camilla, also a painter with a strong bond to her writer sister. Harry and Camilla were clearly modeled on Leonard and Virginia.

As Virginia continued to improve, the publication date for her novel was set for March 26, 1915. She soon relapsed and once again required twenty-four-hour-a-day care. Leonard saw a connection between her mental and physical condition and her fears concerning the public's possible reaction to her work. Like many writers, Virginia found facing critics nearly unbearable. Although E.M. Forster and other highly respected writers and critics had praised her novel, some labeling it a work of genius, Virginia was too ill to comprehend that. She made life unbearable for those around her, often raving and sharply criticizing those she cared about. Leonard Woolf decided to take control.

Decades before the medical community suggested a connection between eating and emotional disorders, Leonard observed that Virginia's diet affected her stability. He took strict control of her food intake. He weighed her daily to be sure that she did not lose weight. He also saw to it that she received rest and regular exercise. For years, he carefully recorded her menstrual periods, as her most severe episodes occurred when her periods became irregular. While many of their friends felt Leonard was too strict and were insulted when he asked visitors to leave when Virginia seemed tired or unwilling to eat, he thought his regimen was necessary to save her life. Once, when he had to be away for a time, Leonard had Virginia sign a contract. She had to agree to rest for a full half-hour following lunch. She was to eat just as she would were he there, to be in bed before 10:30 every night, and to drink a glass of milk each morning.

Leonard also continued to encourage Virginia's writing. Besides wanting to discover new forms for writing fiction, she wanted her writing to reveal aspects of character and experience not usually found in the novel. But she also wanted to be sure that her work was not tinged by her illness. Leonard agreed to read everything she wrote and always reassured her of its quality. Caring for Virginia often exhausted Leonard, but he remained absolutely devoted. After the two terrible bouts of mental illness between 1913 and 1915, she would not suffer another serious episode for twenty-four years.

When they married, Virginia and Leonard agreed that they wanted to support themselves with their writing alone. Before Virginia's bouts of illness this seemed a possibility. Her extensive medical bills depleted their resources and it became harder for the couple to make ends meet.

In June 1914, World War I started in the far-off Balkans, erupting out of a conflict between Russia, Austria-Hungary, and Germany. Two months later, Great Britain was drawn into the fray. Much of Europe would be decimated before the battles came to an end years later.

By early 1915, Leonard had published two books and Virginia's first was on its way. While Leonard's first novel remained a critical success, it produced little income, and his second, *The Wise Virgins,* was both a critical and financial flop. As they awaited the publication of Virginia's first novel, the pair leased Hogarth House in Richmond, a short distance from London. Leonard moved their belongings, checking Virginia into a hospital for medical supervision during his absence. This was the last time he placed her in an institution. In March, *The Voyage Out,* dedicated to Leonard, was released to positive reviews, but it did not become a best seller.

As with several of Virginia's novels, *The Voyage Out* is semi-autobiographical and features a motherless girl, in this case named Rachel Vinrace. The title perhaps reflects Virginia's own voyage from her Hyde Park Gate childhood to the larger adult world. Woolf based Rachel's aunt and uncle, Mr. and Mrs. Ambrose, on her own parents. In the early 1900s, the Ambroses, along with Rachel and her father, Willoughby, depart London on a ship bound for Portugal. Anchoring there, the family remains on board while Willoughby takes care of business in Lisbon. When he returns, he announces they will be joined by Richard and Clarissa Dalloway, an elegant couple who enthrall Rachel. Clarissa reads aloud from Jane Austen's novel *Persuasion* and later gives the book to Rachel. Both Austen's novel and numerous passages in *The Voyage Out* support Virginia's stance on women's suffrage and women's rights in general. At one point in the novel the remark is made that "few things at the present time mattered more than the enlightenment of women." At another, a male character comments, "if I were a woman, I'd blow someone's brains out."

As the plot advances, Rachel, who remains naïve

about sex and in horror of ever having to experience it, feels thrilled, but threatened, when Richard Dalloway kisses her. When her aunt realizes how much Rachel has yet to learn, she asks Willoughby to allow Rachel to travel on to South America with her. He agrees. Rachel eventually falls in love and, while traveling in South America, meets characters that represent various influential people in Virginia Woolf's own life. Suddenly, near the end of the novel, Rachel contracts a fever and dies.

The death of the main character is unusual because Woolf, the author, does not comment on it. Nor does she attempt to neatly resolve the conflicts of the book at its end. Instead, Woolf concludes her novel from the viewpoint of one drowsy character outside the main group, who describes the blurry patterns made by people milling about and the hum of their mingled voices. This ending, a sort of opening out from the narrow focus on the main character, departed from the more traditional approach, which might have had Woolf ending the novel with a commentary on the larger significance of life and death. Virginia's approach reflected the ordinariness of death and people's continued inability to understand it. She did not feel it was the author's job to provide an explanation or a moral. Life and death were simply too large to be captured in so neat a package.

In some ways, this novel reflects Virginia's own conflicts as she struggled with reaching adulthood, deciding about marriage, and navigating women's roles in early twentieth-century society. Some critics have seen it as Woolf's attempt to come to terms with Thoby's death, while others see the relationship between Rachel and the Dalloways as mimicking the relationship between Virginia, Vanessa, and Clive. *The Voyage Out* offers a first glimpse at many political themes that will appear again and again in Virginia's later works. Besides women's rights, these themes included concerns over England's intrusion into other countries as a colonizer, the unethical aspects of war, and poverty.

E.M. Forster, whose opinion was very important to Virginia, praised *The Voyage Out*. He wrote that, although "written by a woman and presumably from a woman's point of view," it "soars straight out of local questionings into the intellectual day." A review in the *Times Literary Supplement* read "never was a book more feminine, more recklessly feminine. It may be labeled clever and shrewd, mocking, suggestive, subtle, 'modern,' but these terms do not convey the spirit of it—which is essentially feminine." Such praise proved crucial to Virginia's confidence, and by the end of 1915 she had began work on her second novel, *Night and Day*.

Chapter Four

The Writing Life

As Virginia's life became more orderly, the world at large descended into chaos. Before staggering to an inconclusive close in 1919, World War I decimated an entire generation of young European men. Most of the men in Virginia's circle of friends were conscientious objectors and refused to fight. The alternative to combat was to appear before a tribunal, which could send the objectors to prison or assign them to some type of work that aided the war, but did not involve actually fighting. The panel might also judge that the objector was not sincerely opposed to war but simply trying to get out of having to fight, in which case he would be forcibly enrolled in the military.

Among those who joined the forces willingly, one of England's most promising young poets, Rupert Brooke, died in battle. Lytton Strachey's medical problems guaranteed he would not have to enlist but he appeared before the tribunal anyway to harass those in charge. John

RUPERT BROOKE
1887–1915

Many lives were lost over the course of the war, including that of poet Rupert Brooke.

Maynard Keynes held a position in the British Treasury that kept him far from the front lines. He supported the war's aims, but declared his sympathy for the pacifists.

Other members of the Stephens' extended family had to make arrangements for service. Clive Bell agreed to work on the farm of a member of Parliament who had declared his opposition to the war. In 1916, Vanessa, by that time totally enthralled with Duncan Grant, moved to a farm with him and one of his former lovers, David Garnett. Both conscientious objectors, the two men performed chores there. Adrian Stephen, a pacifist and lawyer who had recently married a wealthy woman, provided legal defense for the objectors. Leonard could have been called to service, even though he suffered from a hand tremor. But since Virginia's well-being depended on him, her doctor signed a certificate of medical exemption claiming Leonard as her critical caregiver.

In 1916, Roger Fry came to stay with the Woolfs at Hogarth House. He was restoring nine fifteenth-century paintings that were displayed at nearby Hampton Court, one of Henry VIII's favorite palaces. Fry's presence gave Virginia the chance to renew their conversations on the relationship between painting and writing. Fry proposed that aesthetic quality in poetry, or the pleasing aspects of it, resulted purely from a poem's physical form, rather than from the meanings of the words. That form, he insisted, included how the words were arranged on the page, as well as the way they sounded. Virginia wondered whether that idea might also apply to fiction. It was a revolutionary thought, that the physical arrangement of text on the page might influence how a novel affected the reader.

Fry also talked to Virginia about the pain he had suffered when Vanessa rejected him in favor of Duncan Grant. Virginia seemed more accustomed now to both Vanessa's romantic confusion and the separation that had

Staunch pacifists Adrian Stephen and Karin Costelloe were married in 1914, the year that World War I began. *(Photograph from the collection of Angelica Garnett.)*

developed between the two sisters—they had not written each other for some time. When Virginia came down with the flu in April 1916, Vanessa sent a bunch of daffodils that Virginia viewed as a peace offering. She responded quickly, trying to avoid the old patterns of disagreement. She also began to look for a farm near Hogarth House, hoping that Vanessa would relocate.

In July of 1916, the Woolfs visited Vanessa on the Suffolk farm where she lived with Grant and Garnett. Virginia worried somewhat about her sister's living arrangement. She wrote to Lytton Strachey that the farm "seems to lull asleep all ambition," but added optimistically, "Don't you think they have discovered the secret of life? I thought it wonderfully harmonious." Virginia, more than ever, wanted Vanessa close by again, and she urged her sister to move to Richmond, close to Hogarth House. Vanessa agreed, but wanted Grant and Garnett, nicknamed "Bunny," to come too. She found a neighboring farm that needed helpers, and the two men interviewed for the job.

An incident following the interview soured Leonard toward Duncan Grant. When Duncan came for the interview, he brought two art students with him. One of them was a young woman named Dora Carrington, who would later become Lytton Strachey's living companion. Needing a place to sleep that night, Duncan and his companions went to Hogarth House in search of the Woolfs. But Virginia and Leonard were away, so the party broke into their home and spent the night. When they left, Duncan took a book of poetry from Virginia's bedside.

The Woolfs returned home to find their house open, beds slept in, and the book of poetry gone. Worst of all, no one would tell the truth about what had happened. Dora Carrington lied to Virginia about who had taken the book of poetry and had Vanessa help with the cover-up. Leonard feared that having to deal with Vanessa, her children, their household servants, and Grant and Garnett would have a detrimental effect on Virginia's health. They would be living only four miles apart. If Vanessa brought her entourage for a visit it would be an all day affair. Leonard did not want Vanessa's extended family disturbing his and Virginia's peace, or their work. For her sanity, Virginia needed to work.

Virginia, though, welcomed the distraction, especially for the chance to spend time with her young nephews. She did her best to support Vanessa both personally and professionally, purchasing art through a business Vanessa and Grant had started together, called Omega.

Since 1913, Leonard had worked as part-time editor for a magazine called *The New Statesman;* his relationship with the periodical continued for fifty years. In 1916, the chairman, Sidney Webb, asked Woolf to write reviews of war and foreign affairs books. Sidney and his wife, Beatrice, also persuaded Leonard to write two reports for the Fabian Society, a British socialist education society, to which the Webbs belonged.

The Fabians were socialists who rejected Karl Marx's idea that violent revolution was the best means to overthrow the economic system. The Fabians believed society could be made more equitable by peaceful means.

The playwright George Bernard Shaw was an active member of the group and the science fiction writer H.G. Wells had also been a member. A group of intellectuals and writers, the Fabians also promoted the politics of the Labor Party, which was formed in 1900 to represent the working class.

The Woolfs shared the Fabian ideals and Leonard agreed to write two reports calling for the creation of an international authority to intervene in disputes between conflicting nations. The first report appeared in 1915, and in 1916 the Webbs combined the second report with the first into a book titled *International Government,* which would be influential in the development of the League of Nations in 1919. Woolf's ideas were incorporated into a British Draft of the plans for the League. When U.S. President Woodrow Wilson reviewed the draft in Paris, Leonard's statements about labor conditions, public health, and economic and social policy received high praise. Written as Virginia recovered from her 1915 illness, the book was an extraordinary achievement that brought Leonard fame.

Throughout 1917, the fifth year of their marriage, both Woolfs worked with few personal disturbances. Along with the rest of England and the world, though, they wondered whether the war would ever end. They found relief from tension in time spent with family. Although Vanessa called Leonard "the Wolf," because of his close watch over her sister, she and Grant spent happy times with Virginia and Leonard. Like everyone else during the war, they were only able to get rationed portions of food such as meat and sugar, and they celebrated when special foods became available. One September evening Virginia and Leonard picked an abundance of mushrooms, and they shared their treasure with Vanessa and Grant.

As Virginia continued work on *Night and Day,* the Woolfs began a venture that would affect not only their lives, but the future of English literature as well. They decided to start their own press in order to print their works without having to deal with editors and publishers. They also wanted to print work by others. With her instinct for fine writing, Virginia would be the first to publish many burgeoning writers, who would go on to be famous novelists, economists, and politicians. The Woolfs named their press after their beloved Richmond home.

The Hogarth Press's first publication was a pamphlet released in July 1917. Titled *Two Stories,* it contained Virginia's "Mark on the Wall" and Leonard's "Three Jews." "Mark on the Wall" is narrated by a person who contemplates disappearing into a spot on a wall in order to escape reality. Clive thought it "perfect," and Vanessa praised the story too. Purchased mainly by family and friends, the booklet turned a tiny profit. The Woolfs spent their afternoons setting type and printing on their old press, a process that proved to be both time-consuming and rewarding.

Their second publication was a more ambitious undertaking. Few had yet heard of Katherine Mansfield but she would become a celebrated fiction writer before long. The press also printed a book of poems by Leonard's

Katherine Mansfield and Virginia were friends as well as literary rivals.

brother, Cecil N. Sidney Woolf, who had been killed at the battle of Cambrai. The same mortar shell that killed Cecil in December of 1917 wounded another of Woolf's brothers, Philip.

Over the next several years, Hogarth Press printed work by a little-known American who worked in a London bank, T.S. Eliot. Eliot later became one of the most important and influential poets of the twentieth century. Virginia described him as "an American of the highest culture, so that his writing is almost unintelligible." The Woolfs also worked with a Russian named Samuel Kotelianshky, called Kot, and published works by Leo Tolstoy and Anton Chekhov. They published books by E.M. Forster, Edwin Muir, Robert Graves, Rose Macaulay, Edith Sitwell, Gertrude Stein, Hugh Walpole, Rebecca West, H.G. Wells, and two later poet laureates of Britain, C. Day Lewis and John Betjeman. They published the first British editions of three important American poets, John Crowe Ransom, Robinson Jeffers, and Edward Arlington Robinson. Hogarth Press also released translations of works by European writers never before read in English, including the Czech poet Rainer Maria Rilke and the Italian novelist Italo Svevo. They published Philip Noel-Baker, who was later awarded the Nobel Prize for his writing about disarmament;

Poet T.S. Eliot, as drawn by Wyndham Lewis. *(From the Harvard University Portrait Collection.)*

John Maynard Keynes, the most influential economist of his age; and Sigmund Freud, whose theories revolutionized modern thought about human nature and psychology.

A list of the works published by Hogarth Press illustrates the extensive connections the Woolfs had to many of the most creative minds of their age. They put their reputations on the line with each publication, and sophisticated readers came to trust and respect their judgement. Within three years, they had to hire people to help with the busy operation. Many of the employees found Leonard opinionated and stubborn, but most got along just fine with Virginia.

THE HOGARTH PRESS

52 TAVISTOCK SQUARE, LONDON, W.C.1.

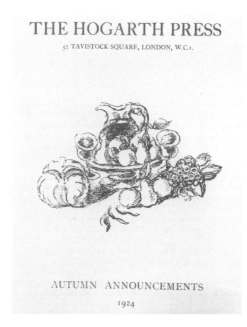

AUTUMN ANNOUNCEMENTS

1924

Hogarth Press was an exciting venture for the Woolfs, allowing them the opportunity to work with some of the most important writers of their generation.

The once difficult and troubled Virginia had improved a great deal. She and Leonard had settled into a devoted relationship, and she and Vanessa continued to be close. Things began to improve globally, as well. The United States entered the war in 1917 and by November 1918, after approximately twenty million deaths, World War I drew to an end. Peace was finally negotiated in 1919.

Vanessa gave the family another reason to celebrate on Christmas Day 1918, with the birth of her third child, a daughter fathered by Duncan Grant. Clive Bell agreed that Vanessa could give the child, named Angelica, his name. Angelica would not learn her father's true identity for years. Having renewed bonds with her sister, Virginia could not ignore the immediate chaos the birth brought into Vanessa's home at nearby Charleston. Angelica was sickly and required a good deal of medical care.

Vanessa's two boys also kept the household in an

uproar. At Virginia's suggestion, Leonard brought the boys to stay with them while the baby was sick. Virginia planned activities to keep the boys occupied. She had noticed Julian's gift for vocabulary, and thought she might teach him Greek, while she hoped to persuade Quentin to be a writer. Unfortunately, after the boys arrived Virginia had to have a tooth pulled and went to bed for eleven days. The boys had to return home, but Leonard loaned Vanessa the Woolfs' servant.

Over the years, Virginia helped Vanessa by showering her with gifts, including money, a refrigerator, and a fur coat. Vanessa could not always return Virginia's attention because of her responsibilities to her children. Bunny Garnett was still living with her and Virginia later learned that Bunny, who provided no financial help to the family, often tried to seduce Vanessa's houseguests. Grant and Bunny Garnett had also resumed their old affair.

Virginia was content with her relatively calm, childless life. At thirty-seven years old, she looked forward to a long and interesting career, and she saw her friend Roger Fry, still energetic and productive at fifty-two, as proof of this possiblity.

In March of 1919, Gerald Duckworth agreed to follow up publication of Virginia's first novel with publication of her second, *Night and Day*. As the novel's release approached, Virginia and Leonard moved to a new home, Monk's House, in the quiet village of Rodmell, in Sussex county near the southern coast. Virginia also kept watch over Vanessa, whose relationship with Duncan Grant continued to unravel. She worked hard at preparing ma-

Vanessa at her home in Charleston, in 1920. *(Photograph from the collection of Angelica Garnett.)*

terials for Hogarth Press, including her short story "Kew Gardens," which was published in May. With this story Virginia began to achieve some of her artistic goals, as she focused the story less on the action and more on the rich and evocative language. Fry approved of her experiment, as did Katherine Mansfield, who by this time reviewed books for a journal called *Athenaeum*. A *Times Literary Supplement* review brimming with praise caused an immediate increase in sales of "Kew Gardens," which bolstered Virginia's self-confidence tremendously. *Night and Day,* dedicated to Vanessa, appeared in November 1919. Like all of Virginia's works, it was born from her own experiences. She intended it to be a playful response to Leonard's novel, *The Wise Virgins.* Virginia said she had fashioned the main character on Vanessa, but later readers would argue that Katharine Hilbery had much more in common with Virginia.

Laced with humor, the novel depicts five young people dealing with problems related to love, work, and marriage. Set in London during the early twentieth century, the characters struggle to escape the judgmental attitudes of the previous generation. It was the last of Woolf's novels to utilize a traditional, linear plot.

In the novel, Katharine Hilbery does not really want to marry, but feels pressured to do so. She has a passion for mathematics, which is considered to be an unusual interest for a female. She keeps her mathematical interest a secret and, in public, conforms to parental and societal demands. Katharine helps her mother write a biography of her grandfather and spends her days waiting to get married. Then she befriends the bold Mary Datchett, who encourages her to throw off society's expectations. Katharine finds her escape in Ralph Denham, a Jewish attorney who is also a writer. Ralph is annoyed with himself for fantasizing about Katharine, a young woman whose Victorian idealism he rejects. After many false starts, Katharine and Ralph at last declare their love and share their secrets. Eventually Katharine confides in her mother, who advises her to marry for love, not social standing. The novel's conflicts are resolved when Katharine and Ralph announce their engagement.

The book was another step in Woolf's struggle to shape her narrative in unprecedented ways. A character from her first novel had hoped to "write a novel about Silence; the things people don't say." Virginia would not achieve that goal until her third novel, but her second book moved her closer.

Night and Day received mixed reviews, with E. M. Forster writing that the characters were so logical that they seemed only one-dimensional. However, the *Times Literary Supplement* said that the humorous novel was filled with wisdom, "so exciting that to read it is to pass through a keen emotional experience." Katherine Mansfield's reaction had the greatest effect on Woolf, when she termed the novel an updating of Jane Austen. Though Mansfield meant it as a compliment, Virginia thought this was a terrible insult. She had wanted to create something entirely new.

Later critics, who see the novel in the continuum of Woolf's work, have noted that in *Night and Day* she reduces emphasis on the events of the plot and focuses instead on the symbols of light and dark, as suggested by the novel's title, to convey the idea that opposites can complement one another to produce a perfect whole. In the final union of Katharine and Ralph, Virginia suggests one androgynous creature (neither purely masculine or feminine, but having the qualities of both).

Virginia later said that she had learned much from writing *Night and Day* and would avoid its problems in her future work. The rest of her novels would focus on women and their shifting positions in society as revealed through family relationships. Her next novel, *Jacob's Room,* would achieve her longtime goal of devising a truly revolutionary approach to writing fiction.

Part of the aftermath of World War I was a reconciliation between the Bloomsbury Group and John Maynard Keynes. His work for the government had caused many of his pacifist friends to renounce him because they believed he supported the war. However, his 1919 book, *Economic Consequences of Peace,* proved to them that he had not abandoned his ethics after all. In it, he explained and examined the ways the Allies had profited from war. He specifically criticized the Treaty of Versailles (the 1919 treaty that formally ended World War I) for forcing Germany to accept full responsibility for starting the war, even though it had actually grown out of a number of conflicts over land and resources. The treaty stripped Germany of much of its most valuable territory and demanded the nation make huge reparations (punitive financial payments). Keynes argued that the treaty set up conditions that would inevitably give rise to another European war, which is exactly what would happen two decades later, when Adolf Hitler rose to power in Germany and Benito Mussolini became dictator of Italy. The treaty, Keynes warned, also did little to incorporate the new communist government of the Soviet Union into the world community. The publication of *Economic Consequences of Peace* helped to rehabilitate Keynes's reputation in the eyes of the Bloomsbury Group.

As one friendship was mended, another was lost when, the following year, Virginia parted ways with Madge Vaughan, the cousin who had once been so important to her. Madge had wanted to rent Vanessa's home while the family was away, but declared she could not do so until making it clear to Vanessa that she disapproved of Angelica's illegitimacy. Both Vanessa and Virginia were outraged and immediately ended contact with Madge, as they had done with other family and friends who voiced disapproval of their lifestyles.

In 1920, Leonard published *Empire and Commerce in Africa,* one of the first major works to insist that nations that colonized other countries should treat the colonized people fairly and humanely. Leonard followed this success with his final fictional work, *Stories from the East.* A fifty-five-page volume of three tales, its cover decorated with a woodcut by Dora Carrington, the little book garnered critical praise. Editors approached Leonard about revising the stories to make them publishable in the United States, by which they meant that he should modulate his brutal honesty about race and gender relations, caste systems, and imperialism. He refused their requests, and the book was never published in the United States.

That same year, Virginia enjoyed a smaller victory of her own when she made her first public address. Through her continued conversations with Roger Fry regarding the nature of art, she became interested in Sigmund Freud's psychological theories. She wrote an article about studies that had attempted to distinguish between the artistic and scientific sides of the human brain. This was the first of many presentations to come.

Virginia and Leonard had decided to place her new novel, *Jacob's Room,* with a new publisher. They feared that Gerald Duckworth might make editorial changes in an attempt to force the novel into a more traditional mold. Virginia prepared her readers to expect an experimental novel from her when she wrote in one of her *Times Literary Supplement* reviews that the novel must "change and develop as it is explored by the most vigorous minds of a very complex age."

When *Jacob's Room* appeared in October, it was obvious to most critics that Virginia Woolf was an innovative literary force. That did not mean, however, that they liked the novel. An attempt to base a narrative on the way the human mind operates, *Jacob's Room* presents the reader with impressions of its main character arranged in no particular order. Because it departed from the familiar linear plot, many readers and critics found it difficult to read and its meaning obscure. The *Times Literary Supplement* praised Virginia for being adventurous, but summarized, "it does not create persons and characters as we secretly desire to know them." Others termed it "reproachfully post-impressionist." Some later critics labeled *Jacob's Room* a "prose-poem," no more than a loving tribute to Thoby Stephen who had died sixteen years earlier. Jacob does not often speak, instead, readers learn about him from his thoughts as he seeks to live his life vicariously through those around him. Despite its mixed critical reception, the book sold well enough that it had to be reprinted two years later. It was also published in America.

Virginia soon settled down to focus on her next novel, *Mrs. Dalloway,* and to write a collection of essays on literature titled *The Common Reader.* She temporarily gave up writing reviews to focus all her energy on her

Virginia began a romantic affair with Vita Sackville-West in 1922. *(Radio Times Hulton Picture Library.)*

own work. Her decision was made easier by the financial security provided by Leonard's new position as literary editor of the *Nation*.

Mrs. Dalloway may have been inspired by a romantic affair Virginia began in 1922 with Vita Sackville-West, a writer herself, and a fan of Virginia's work. Their affair would continue until Virginia's death many years later. It is likely, though, that inspriation for the novel came when Virginia was reminded of the fragile, temporary nature of life by Katherine Mansfield's unexpected death on January 9, 1923. Virginia's January 16 diary entry reflects her feelings regarding the death of the author she had published and admired:

> At that one feels—what? A shock of relief?—a rival the less? Then confusion at feeling so little—then, gradually, blankness & disappointment; then a depression which I could not rouse myself from all that day. When I began to write, it seemed to me there was no point in writing. Katherine wont [sic] read it. Katherine's my rival no longer . . . thought I can do this better than she could, where is she, who could do what
> I can't!

She adds, "For two days I felt that I had grown middle aged, & lost some spur to write." With the help of Leonard, Virginia overcame those feelings. She did begin writing again, fighting the "certain melancholy" that Katherine's death had inflicted upon her.

Chapter Five

"A Room of One's Own"

By 1923, buoyed by the confidence gained from the success of Hogarth Press and the positive reaction to so much of her own writing, Virginia was ready to publicly discuss her ideas on writing and art. A July diary entry reads, "Never settle, is my principle in life." Her new confidence was summarized in the bold statement, "unless I am myself, I am nobody."

While visiting Vanessa's Charleston home in early September, Virginia was heard joking that Vanessa, Duncan, and Roger were so focused on their paintings that they were ignoring their guests. Yet, she no longer seemed upset by this sort of behavior, which she would once have thought intentionally hurtful. It seemed Virginia had overcome her paranoia and low self-esteem.

During that year, Virginia's sense of humor helped her family and friends through some difficult times. Adrian filed for a divorce from his wife, Karin, which dampened everyone's spirits. Virginia was particularly upset because Adrian's analyst had told him that his childhood and upbringing were to blame for the failure of his marriage. Virginia hoped to lift everyone's spirits with a play called *Freshwater,* a comic rendition of the life of their great aunt, the photographer Julia Margaret Cameron. Virginia had planned to finish it by the family Christmas party, but could not. Instead she entertained everyone by writing, along with her nephew Quentin, a farce based on Vanessa's life. It left Vanessa collapsed in laughter.

The Woolfs returned to live in London, although they continued to rent Monk's House to visit at their leisure. Once again they were in the middle of their circle of friends and family, many of whom lived close by at Gordon Square. Adrian's ex-wife Karin remained in their old home and Clive lived upstairs from her. Vanessa lived a few doors down, with Keynes upstairs, and Adrian boarded with members of Lytton Strachey's family another few houses away.

Virginia began January 1924 by writing in her diary that change was a good, if painful, thing: "Youth is a matter of forging ahead. I see my contemporaries satisfied, outwardly; inwardly conscious of emptiness." She seemed hopeful, writing "I should like, very much, to turn the last page of this virgin volume & there find my dreams come true."

Leonard and Virginia's life continued to change. He cut back on the time he spent working at the *Nation.* He published one full-length book and a collection of essays over the next several years. Most of his time went to supporting Virginia and running Hogarth Press.

Virginia's prediction of an eventful and productive year proved true. Determined to complete *Mrs. Dalloway* by September, and her book of essays soon after, Virginia wrote furiously. In May she read her essay, "Character in Fiction," at Cambridge University, and a revision of that essay later became the first in a new series of pamphlets published by the Woolfs, titled *Hogarth Essays.* Roger Fry would contribute the next essay in the series.

Virginia's relationship with Vita Sackville-West continued to develop and the women exchanged numerous letters. Vita made no secret of her attraction to Virginia, but Virginia was shy, initially showing her interest only in Vita's work. Vita agreed to write a piece for Hogarth to publish.

Leonard spent the summer meeting once a week with the Labor Party's leaders. He was increasingly frustrated that, while all of them came from the working class, none of them had any background in economics or international affairs. He bemoaned the fact that they failed to bring about any important reforms. Virginia became more convinced than ever that only art could save the world.

By September of 1924, Virginia was close to finishing her novel, which concluded with a party scene. She wrote that she was in her "last lap of Mrs. D. There I am now—at last at the party, which is to begin in the kitchen, & climb slowly upstairs. It is to be a most complicated spirited, solid piece, knitting together everything & ending on three notes."

Although pleased with the novel, Virginia braced herself for criticism from those who still expected fiction to adhere to conventional forms. Determined to enjoy the remainder of the year, she planned another Christmas celebration, during which Virginia again teamed with her nephew Quentin, this time to write the "Dunciad." Borrowing the name from a satiric poem by Alexander Pope

Virginia enjoyed Quentin's company and encouraged his writing. Together, they collaborated on a number of lighthearted plays for family gatherings. *(Photograph from the collection of Quentin Bell.)*

about dullards who attempted to write literature in the eighteenth century, their work was again a comedy, but this one was about Duncan Grant. The group enjoyed it immensely.

As they waited for the publication of *Mrs. Dalloway,* the Woolfs kept busy with Hogarth Press. In 1925, they printed T. S. Eliot's masterpiece, *The Wasteland,* and Kot's translations of Russian authors, along with the *Collected Papers of Sigmund Freud.* The press even made enough money to allow them to visit Vanessa in France.

Virginia's book of essays, *The Common Reader,* came out on April 23, 1925, followed by *Mrs. Dalloway* on May 14. *The Common Reader* delighted the public; like all of Virginia's essays, the collection masked sharp and sophisticated literary criticism with a deceptively simple style. Her novel, though, proved not nearly as accessible. It consists of two parallel stories that take place in a single day, and concerns itself with theme rather than action. Its two main characters are only thinly connected by coincidence and the novel forces readers to contemplate large and difficult questions, including the meaning of life.

The book focuses in part on Clarissa Dalloway (Mrs. Dalloway), a socialite who is hosting a party the prime minister will attend. The second main character, Septimus Smith, is a shell-shocked war veteran who will commit suicide by the day's end. Clarissa spends part of the day immersed in memories, including that of an old lover, Peter Walsh. Peter and Clarissa have an unexpected encounter which leads Clarissa to reconsider the path her life has taken. At the same time, Septimus's wife, Rezia, takes him to visit a nerve specialist, Dr. William Bradshaw. The two stories overlap briefly during Clarissa's party when Dr. Bradshaw mentions Septimus to Clarissa's husband, the politician Richard Dalloway, who is at work on a bill in Parliament to help veterans suffering from

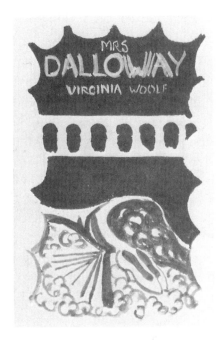

Vanessa designed the cover of Virginia's novel, *Mrs. Dalloway. (Photo. by Eileen Tweedy.)*

trauma related to the war. Besides this, the two stories seem to have no connection. But beneath the surface, they reflect and comment on each other. The tenuous and complex relationship between the novel's two main characters proved to be challenging for Virginia's readers.

Virginia drew from her own experiences when writing the scenes portraying madness. For instance, Septimus hears birds speaking Greek, just as she had, and he has other delusions similar to hers. Septimus symbolizes the horrors of war, and his death reminds the reader of the bleakness that pervaded Europe for many years after World War I's end.

In her depiction of London, Woolf is both effusive and critical. She wrote in her diary, "We walk home from theatres, through the entrails of London. Why do I love it so much? . . . for it is stony hearted and callous." The entry continues, "Indeed most of life escapes, now I come to think of it; the texture of the ordinary day." This texture is what manages to enrich the gloom, and Woolf hoped her novel might capture it. *Mrs. Dalloway* was the first to suggest that a great story could be told in a small way.

As well, *Mrs. Dalloway* was Woolf's first truly mature work. It heralded her move from the more traditional structure of *The Voyage Out* to the experimental narratives she would use in her later novels, including *The Waves* and *To the Lighthouse*.

The wide variety of reactions to *Mrs. Dalloway* pleased Virginia. Selling more than eight thousand copies in England and the United States in 1925, it almost doubled the sales of *Jacob's Room*. *The Common Reader* proved so successful that Virginia decided to write another volume of essays. Thomas Hardy, another revolutionary novelist of the time, publicly praised her work, and when Roger Fry attended a literary convention in France, he found the participants in awe of Virginia's talent.

By the end of the year, Virginia and Vita Sackville-West were engaged in a heartfelt and erotic correspondence. Vita was married to Harold Nicolson, a diplomat, but both she and her husband preferred to have intimate relationships with members of their own gender. Vita had joined her husband in Persia, but she and Virginia continued their correspondence.

Virginia Woolf at the peak of her creative powers, in 1927. *(Photo. by Marianne Beck for* Vogue.*)*

If 1925 had been an important year for Virginia, 1926 proved crucial. Her writing was now earning her larger and larger sums of money, and those amounts increased dramatically from one year to the next. In 1926, she would also produce the novel that remains one of her most popular, *To the Lighthouse*.

When Vita returned to England in May of 1926, she spent time with Virginia at Monk's House. She thought that Virginia looked unhealthy, but Virginia seemed to feel fine. Virginia accepted an invitation to meet Gertrude Stein, an American writer who often hosted artists in her Paris home. Stein acted as a sponsor and confidant for several American writers, including Ernest Hemingway and Sherwood Anderson. Virginia found her fascinating. That year the Woolfs enjoyed several excursions, visiting, for one, the aging Thomas Hardy, who misspelled Virginia's last name when signing her copy of *Life's Little Ironies*. She suffered from a slight depression in July, but recovered quickly under Vita's care. She continued to work on her new novel and found inspiration in her conversations with Roger Fry.

Fry had once made a simplified, cubist version of a Raphael painting of the Christ child that provoked hostile public reaction. Virginia had always thought his painting was a heroic act. In *To the Lighthouse,* when she has a character who is also an artist paint the Madonna and child as a purple triangle, Virginia is paying homage to her painter friend. When another character realizes that the shape of the object does not detract from the reverence in which artists hold their subjects, Virginia hopes her readers will come to the same realization. She drew a figure in her diary, two blocks joined by a corridor, that represented Roger's idea of balance in art. Her novel took the same form, with two traditional narratives joined by a nontraditional midsection titled simply "Time Passes."

In the fall of 1926, Virginia struggled to complete the new novel. Another wave of depression threatened to halt her progress completely in September. Frustrated, she wrote that she hated her body and her mind because she

The central image, and symbol, of Virginia's novel *To the Lighthouse* was inspired by her childhood visits to this lighthouse near Talland House. *(Photograph by Ann James.)*

had so little control over them. By November, she had stopped her diary entries completely in order to finish *To the Lighthouse,* but she still found time to spend with Vita.

In early 1927, when Vanessa traveled to France to care for Duncan Grant, who was ill, Virginia was left to muse on the importance of their close relationship. She and her sister would continue to argue, but they came to realize how much they needed each other.

To the Lighthouse was based on Virginia's memories of the Stephen family's escapes to the ocean when she was a child. In the book, Virginia developed a series of images depicting the fictional Ramsey family in various groupings, always anchored by the view of a lighthouse across the bay. The novel's Mr. and Mrs. Ramsey clearly represent Julia and Leslie Stephen, and also have eight children. Despite their personal failings, Mr. and Mrs. Ramsey tie the family together with strong bonds of love. The lighthouse symbolizes different things to each of the novel's characters. It offers the promise of adventure to the children, the idea of control to the father, and is the center of the mother's vision of her family. For the lighthouse keeper and his handicapped son, it is a place to live and work.

The novel does not follow a logical, time-directed structure, and it hints at more than it clearly identifies. Its rhythm reflects the ebb and flow of the sea. While reviews at the time of its release were mixed, *To the Lighthouse* outsold all of Virginia's previous books. The public responded positively to Virginia's continued experiments with the way a story could be told, the way a novel could be written.

Leonard had labeled *To the Lighthouse* "a psychological poem," and declared it to be something very new in fiction. Roger Fry stated it was by far the best of Virginia's writings. E. M. Forster declared it "very beautiful both in (non-radiant) colour and shape, it stirs me much more to questions of whether and why than anything else you have written."

When Virginia completed the novel in February 1927, she wanted to push on to her next project. The recent death of her cousin Madge reminded her of her own mortality. Virginia wondered how many more books she would write. Even though she believed biography to be the most difficult type of writing to do well, she decided that her next book would be a type of biography and would cover vast amounts of time.

Virginia titled the new book *Orlando: A Biography,* and based it on the life of Vita Sackville-West. Because she distrusted the way biographers could manipulate facts, Virginia decided to parody the biographical form. The book begins with an ironic preface mimicking that of the familiar biography and thanking her many influences, including Sir Walter Scott, Emily Brontë, and Walter Pater. It also acknowledges the help of everyone in her inner circle, including her young nephew Quentin Bell, "an old and valued collaborator in fiction." *Orlando* is almost entirely fabrication, right down to the photographs it contains that claim to be of characters mentioned in the text, including "The Russian Princess as a Child," for which Angelica Bell posed.

Virginia created the character Orlando, who lives for hundreds of years and, along the way, transforms from a man to a woman. Virginia wanted to illustrate to her readers how drastically women have been oppressed throughout history. One incident she had in mind was the fact that Vita had not been able to inherit her beloved home from her father due to a law dictating that all property must pass to a man.

Many critics dismissed the 1928 novel; one called it "a high-brow lark." But others, such as the American writer Rebecca West, called *Orlando* "a poetic masterpiece." She praised Virginia's contempt for realism. Later critics have seen it as an important feminist work. Once again, Virginia's work proved extremely popular, with the first printings in England and America of about twelve thousand copies selling out quickly.

The same year that *Orlando* appeared, Virginia was invited to give a talk to the Arts Society of Newnham College (the women's college at Cambridge University) on the subject of "Women and Fiction." She used the opportunity to point out the great differences between colleges for women and those for men. The women's college had small, dark rooms, which were mostly undecorated. In a diary entry, she compared the corridors to "vaults in some horrid high church cathedral . . . cold & shiny." She had recently enjoyed a sumptuous meal with a male friend at King's College, part of Oxford University, and she could not help but compare it to the meager food served at the women's school.

In her lectures, Woolf asked her audience to pretend that William Shakespeare, the most talented writer in the English language, had an equally talented sister named Judith. She asked the group whether Judith might have become as celebrated as her brother, then answered her own question with a resounding "No."

Woolf went on to explain why: Judith would have found no encouragement for her desire to write. In fact, she probably would not have even learned to read or write. If she had been fortunate enough to gain an education and write the plays that lived in her imagination, audiences would never have seen them performed. Acting groups did not buy material written by women. Had she run away to London, like William, to try to bring her work to the stage herself, she would have failed. English laws forbade women to appear on the stage. However, Virginia added, her audience had a chance to redeem Judith: "But she lives, for great poets do not die; they are continuing presences; they need only the opportunity to walk among us in the flesh."

In her diary Virginia described the young women in her audience as "starved but valiant . . . intelligent, eager, poor," and facing dull futures as schoolmistresses in poor neighborhoods. She knew the only way their futures could improve was if they worked for change. She told them to "drink wine & have a room of their own," a call to independence many of these young women had never before heard. When her lectures appeared as the 1929 book, *A Room of One's Own,* the message went international. The book immediately sold 22,000 copies and gained status as a feminist work that called for a quiet revolution among women writers.

On November 28, 1928, Leslie Stephen's birthday, Virginia began her diary entry by reflecting that her father would have been ninety-six-years old. She went on to consider her own mortality. Her writing was at a standstill, and she wrote that she would have to wait to write until her next idea had "grown heavy in my mind like a ripe pear . . . asking to be cut . . . The Moths still haunts me." ("The Moths" refers to a story idea that would eventually grow into a book titled *The Waves*.)

Near the end of 1928, Virginia and Leonard visited Vita and her husband in Germany. Virginia became ill again when she returned home. Her final January 1929 diary entry noted her feeling of being "haunted" by two contradictions. One was the permanence of life in general, the other that individual lives were "transitory, flying, diaphanous. I shall pass like a cloud on the waves." Much of her work centers around dichotomies like this one. She was forever fascinated by images (like the mysterious fin rising out of the water) that could be both promising and foreboding.

Virginia remained sick in bed for three weeks. When she returned to the diary in March, she reflected on what she seemed to think of as her duties as a writer: "One ought perhaps to be forever finding new things to say, since life draws on. One ought to invent a fine narrative style." The entry ends on a hopeful note as she writes, "even if I see ugliness in the glass . . . inwardly I am more full of shape & colour than ever. I think I am bolder as a writer . . . I feel on the verge of some strenuous adventure." In the coming years she would produce not just one more novel, but four.

Virginia's income increased enough in 1929 to allow Leonard to quit his job. In 1930, the Woolfs spent most of their time at Monk's House, where Leonard worked on publishing projects with Hogarth Press and a book of his own, *After the Deluge*. He hoped to begin a book series that would help people understand the causes of war, in an effort to prevent another one. Meanwhile, Virginia was working on her seventh novel, *The Waves*.

Chapter Six

The Best and the Worst

On January 26, 1930, Virginia Woolf wrote in her diary that her work on *The Waves* made her feel "like a fly on gummed paper." She predicted the novel would not sell even 2,000 copies. Over the next ten years, pessimism slowly regained control of her mind.

On New Year's Eve, the Woolfs attended Vanessa's party for Angelica, by this time twelve years old, and everyone came dressed as a character from *Alice in Wonderland*. Following the party, the Woolfs came upon a scene that perfectly represented the kind of social injustice Leonard hated. Two men had been harassing a middle-aged woman who had been drinking. When the police arrived on the scene, the men ran, but the woman could not get away. The police were goading the woman when Leonard stepped between them. He told the police they ought to find the men who were really to blame, rather than picking on this woman. Mrs. Maynard Keynes happened to be outside her house nearby and later reported her amazement at what she saw. There stood Leonard, costumed as *Alice in Wonderland's* Carpenter in a paper hat and green apron, and Virginia, wearing her March Hare ears and paws, scolding the police.

Writing a book was always a difficult emotional process for Virginia, particularly as it neared completion. In February, Virginia wrote that she felt doors were opening in her novel and "the moth [was] shaking its wings in me." In late March she declared, "children are nothing to this," aptly seeing her writing as a sort of birthing process, complete with the difficult, sometimes painful labor before the final release. By April, Virginia felt that the end was near, and claimed she could "see the last lap straight ahead."

The Woolfs spent much of 1930 in the country, where Virginia could write with few distractions. Back in London in January 1931, an idea suddenly came to her as she lounged in the bathtub. She envisioned a follow-up to *A Room of One's Own* titled *Professions for Women,* the name of the speech she would deliver the following day to the National Society for Women's Service. The speech contained her famous story of needing to kill the "angel of the house" before she could become an honest and focused writer. The "angel of the house" referred to the Victorian ideal that women should serve others and take no time for themselves. The new nonfiction project rekindled her imagination, and by February, she had completed *The Waves.*

With *The Waves,* Virginia broke still more new ground. This novel focused on the lives of three men and three

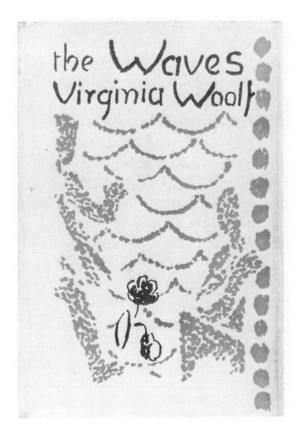

Vanessa designed many of the covers of Virginia's books, including this one for her novel
The Waves. *(Photograph by Eileen Tweedy.)*

women. A seventh character, based on Thoby Stephen,
has a relationship with all six, and an important part of
each of their stories is based on that friendship. Written
in nine episodes separated by descriptions of time pass-
ing from morning to night, the novel was rooted in the
vision of the fin Virginia had seen in 1926, the fin that
could symbolize either hope or death, depending on the

creature it belonged to. Virginia thought of this novel as the center of a flower, the only part remaining when the petals have fallen away. She called her final draft a "series of dramatic soliloquies" timed to the rhythm of waves.

Hogarth Press published the novel in October in England and it appeared in the United States just two weeks later. Vanessa designed the front and back jacket and the artwork on the spine. The novel's theme of alienation as part of the human condition echoes Virginia's other works. Although she predicted the novel would fail, critics appreciated its structure, the beautifully chosen words, and the powerful imagery.

After finishing *The Waves,* Virginia began another project titled *Flush,* a biography based on the life of Elizabeth Barrett Browning's cocker spaniel. The dog had served as a topic for three of Browning's sonnets. For the book, Virginia used her own cocker spaniel, Pinka, as her model. Browning was one of England's most beloved poets, who had relocated to Italy, where she campaigned for human rights. Virginia hoped to provide an ironic insight into the poet's life by telling her story from the point of view of a dog. A few months later, she also began work on a book she initially titled *The Pargiters,* which was another demanding project. *Flush* provided relief from the more serious novel.

Virginia promised Leonard she would rest through the month of December. On the tenth, she wrote a letter to Lytton Strachey, whom she had not seen in some time. She had followed his writing career, however, and at times felt jealous of his work. Now Strachey was ill, and by the time Virginia's letter arrived he had become critically so. On Christmas Eve, the Woolfs received word that he was beyond hope, and they cried together, talking again of aging and death. By the next day, though, Strachey seemed better, and on January 14, 1932, the Woolfs drove to his home. They visited with a very distracted Dora Carrington, who was Strachey's devoted caretaker in his final years, but did not get to see Lytton.

Considering how sick their good friend was, Vanessa wondered whether she should hold a party planned for January 21. When Lytton's brother notified friends that he seemed better, they decided to go ahead. But the guests arrived to find Vanessa, Virginia, and Duncan Grant sobbing together; Lytton Strachey had died that very day.

When Virginia spoke with Dora Carrington, she had the impression that Dora was thinking of suicide. Having made two suicide attempts herself, Virginia told Dora that she understood her feelings of hopelessness. The Woolfs received word the next evening that Dora Carrington had shot herself. Virginia wondered if there was anything she could have said to Dora to help her want to live. In the end, she had no answer.

Soon thereafter, Cambridge University invited Virginia to deliver the prestigious Clark lectures. She turned the offer down. Had she accepted, she would have been given an honorary doctorate degree and followed in her father's steps as a Clark lecturer. Despite the chance to live up to her father's memory, Virginia remained angry at the second-class treatment women received at England's more prestigious schools and did not want to be forced to conform to the restrictions imposed on professors.

Needing something to rejuvenate them, Virginia and Leonard left England in April, with Roger Fry and his sister Margery, to visit Greece. All four enjoyed the trip. Margery and Roger seemed to know everything about the "art, architecture, folk-lore, fauna, flora, geography, geology and history of Greece." Leonard and Virginia relaxed and let Roger act as their tour guide.

The feeling of relaxation they returned home with was short-lived. Tension was high at the busy Hogarth Press and, after a heated argument with Leonard, several employees quit. Then a critic published a hostile review of Virginia's work. By the end of May she was again filled with despair and self-doubt.

In spite of this, her writing went well, although she worked on little besides nonfiction until the fall. In July, she published "A Letter to a Young Poet" as the eighth in *The Hogarth Letters* series.

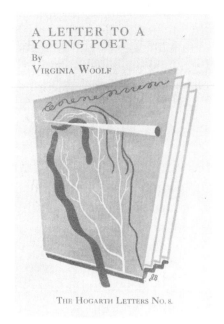

A LETTER TO A
YOUNG POET
By
VIRGINIA WOOLF

THE HOGARTH LETTERS NO. 8.

Virginia Woolf's "Letter to a Young Poet." *(Cover designed by John Banting.)*

The Second Common Reader, another collection of critical essays, appeared in October. It quickly went into a second printing. After almost nine months away from it, she finally returned to *Flush* and finished the next-to-last chapter.

By the fall, Virginia had returned to *The Pargiters* and planned to make it the most traditional novel she had written since *Night and Day*. Her nephew later compared watching her joyful exhaustion as she worked on that book to watching her "run gaily and swiftly out onto quicksand." Virginia finished *Flush* in early 1933 and then turned all of her attention to *The Pargiters*.

When *Flush* appeared in October, it was wildly popular. The first printing was the largest of any of her first editions and was followed by several reprintings. Virginia was amused by the amount of mail she received from dog lovers—readers she thought had clearly misunderstood the book.

In early 1934, Virginia had an explosion of creativity during which she created the great air-raid scene in *The Pargiters*. Exhausted by the effort, the Woolfs took a brief holiday in Ireland once she recovered. They arrived during a rainy late April and enjoyed a calm and pleasant stay until Leonard opened a London newspaper and read an obituary for George Duckworth.

Virginia recorded her thoughts about her half brother's death in her diary. George represented her childhood, "the batting, the laughter, the treats, the presents, taking us for bus rides to see famous churches, giving us tea at City Inns, & so on—that was the best." She concluded

Vanessa designed the above endpaper for Virginia's book *Flush,* her whimsical biography of Elizabeth Barrett Browning's cocker spaniel. *(Photograph by Eileen Tweedy.)*

her entry by thinking of how far away England seemed as she sat by the windy sea, waiting for her evening meal, "with this usual sense of time shifting & life becoming unreal, so soon to vanish while the world will go on."

A month later, Virginia's words seemed prophetic. In Germany, politicians and businessmen who did not support the recently installed dictatorship of Adolf Hitler were pulled from their beds and murdered in the middle of the night. The disturbing incident caused people to worry where this violence would lead. Maynard Keynes had predicted a second world war would follow quickly on the heels of the first, and his predictions were beginning to come true.

Virginia returned to London hoping to work on her novel, which she had renamed *Here and Now*. By May 22, she wrote that she had tried to "strike the match," and "a little flame" responded. She continued about her characters, "I'm still miles outside them, but I think I got into the right tone of voice."

In September came news that brought everything in Virginia's life to an immediate halt. Roger Fry—the eldest member of the Bloomsbury Group, her confidant for decades, her teacher about all things artistic, and Vanessa's ex-lover—had died of heart failure. Crushed, Virginia wrote: "I think the poverty of life now is what comes to me; and this blackish veil over everything." She attempted to ease her pain by writing a biography of Fry.

Virginia began 1935 with plans to focus on two projects: finishing her novel, which now had its tenth title, *The Years,* and reading all of Fry's correspondence in preparation to write his biography. Leonard planned a project of his own titled *Quack, Quack*. The book was intended to sound a warning about the alarming political and social developments taking place in Germany and Italy.

Virginia finished *The Years* by July and spent the next months revising. She hoped to begin reading Fry's correspondence, but first she had to obtain the letters that Vanessa had kept from the time of their affair. Vanessa was reluctant to turn them over, since some of them were critical of Virginia. In the end, Virginia convinced her

Virginia Woolf in 1935. *(Photograph from the collection of Angelica Garnett.)*

sister she would handle the letters carefully and remain loyal to the truth. In the meantime, some members of Lytton Strachey's family were jealous that Virginia would consider writing about Fry, but not Strachey. Virginia wanted to write about him, but worried some over how she would handle the subject of his homosexuality.

Leonard and Virginia took a trip to Germany and Italy in May 1935 that convinced them that war was inevitably approaching. The anti-Jewish literature they saw in Germany chilled them both, particularly in light of Leonard's Jewish heritage. Leonard looked forward to returning home to his beloved gardens at Monk's House and to their dog Pinka. When they arrived home, however, they found that Pinka had died. By July they had found a replacement of sorts in a black and white cocker spaniel,

Sally, who instantly adored Leonard. Virginia continued revising her novel, reducing its length by almost twenty-five percent.

Working on Fry's biography, Virginia was dismayed to find that he had been romantically involved with so many people. She also began work on another book of nonfiction, *Three Guineas*. She devoted mornings to it and took notes for Roger's biography in the afternoon. She also continued to revise *The Years*. She had spent over a year simply rewriting her novel, and in January of 1936 declared she was sick of fiction.

At last, in 1936, *The Years* went off to the publisher in sections. Leonard helped to proofread it and, having grown used to his encouragement in the past, Virginia was hurt when he did not praise this latest work. She swore she would never write fiction again.

Chapter Seven

New Wars

During the first half of 1936, Virginia kept careful watch over her own health. She and Leonard spent two restful months in the country, but she was unable to sleep. She wrote to friends that she often thought of suicide. She also admitted that she sometimes exaggerated, so no one could tell how serious she was. She took a break from making diary entries but continued to correspond with friends and family. Virginia told her nephew Julian she hoped he might one day explode the traditional style of writing fiction, even though most critics had declared that Virginia had already accomplished that feat. She felt better in June, but by the fall, her depression returned.

Plagued by headaches, Virginia began to feel all of her old doubts regarding her abilities and talent. Her emotional state was serious enough that Leonard praised *The Years* more than he might have otherwise. Virginia cut the manuscript ruthlessly, eliminating any parts that seemed preachy. She tried to adhere to the ideal that the aesthetics of art was more important than its intellectual impact. She removed references to women's sexuality that the reading public might see as taboo, then wondered whether she should have left them in. Trying to uphold her aesthetic values, she sacrificed some of her political ones.

Virginia also began worrying about her nephew Julian. He had asked her and Leonard to publish an essay he had written about Roger Fry, but they had refused. Virginia had not heard from him since. In November, Vanessa told Virginia of a nightmare she had that Julian had died.

While *The Years* was at the printer's, the Woolfs shared a Christmas meal with the Keyneses and spent New Year's with Vanessa, where no one discussed Julian's memoir about Roger. Virginia had finally heard from her nephew and had written to say that she was sorry for hurting him.

For a short period in January of 1937, Virginia again felt happy with her work, although waiting for her novel's publication made her restless. On the weekend of its March debut, she and Leonard visited Vanessa's family. They learned that Julian had come home determined to go to Spain to fight the fascists who were trying to overthrow the elected government. Despite their support of his political beliefs, Vanessa and the Woolfs begged him to reconsider and look for a job in London.

The Years was released and early reviews were quite good. It was an easier read than some of her earlier work and it sold well. Part of its success was due to the popularity of historical chronicles at the time, even though Virginia departed from the traditional historical novel. The actions of her characters emphasized the clash between the beliefs of conservative Victorian culture and the more liberal views of modern culture.

Virginia emphasizes several themes in the novel, including the need for gender equity, the value of human dignity, and the ineffectiveness of violence to achieve change. She likely based her fictional civic group on the Women's Social and Political Union, an organization that used violent protest to push for women's rights. Virginia's friend, Ethel Smyth, had been sent to prison for the actions she took supporting women's rights. Several of her experiences appear in the novel. One character, Rose Pargiter, goes to jail for throwing a brick during a suffrage march, and another character worries that she is being force fed while there, something that happened to many suffragettes.

After the first rush of positive criticism, some negative criticism followed. One reviewer sneered that the novel had obviously been written by a woman unable to deal with reality. Other critics felt Virginia included too much detail with no way for readers to absorb it. Regardless of critical reaction, the novel topped the bestseller list, receiving praise in the United States, where her portrait appeared on the cover of *Time* magazine.

Then on July 20, Julian Bell, who had made good on his promise to fight in Spain's civil war, was killed while driving an ambulance there. As Virginia tried to comfort a devastated Vanessa, she compared the loss of Julian to that of Roger. Both left tremendous gaps in her life. She and Leonard moved to Monk's House for the rest of the summer and transferred Vanessa from London to her nearby country house at Charleston.

Vanessa later wrote that she remembered only Virginia's voice, attempting to keep her afloat, during the next several weeks. Moved by the loss of her son, Vanessa decided at last to explain to Angelica that Duncan Grant, not Clive Bell, was her father. The confession seemed to ease Vanessa's feelings about the loss of Julian, although Angelica angrily accused Vanessa of depriving her of having any father.

Virginia hoped to engage Vanessa's interest in her work on the biography of Roger Fry, and her ploy succeeded. She tried to lose herself in her writing and by October 12, 1937, she had finished *Three Guineas*.

Virginia's new book expressed her frustration over society's negative view of working women. It also took a stand against what she thought of as the male tendency toward militarism. The guinea had originated in the seventeenth century on the African Guinea Coast as a gold coin, but the government had halted its production for more than one hundred years. Even after the gold coin was no longer circulated, the term "guinea" referred to the British coin value of £1 sterling, plus one shilling. People used the term "guinea" when talking about the purchase of luxurious or unnecessary items.

Virginia used the guinea to suggest the high value of three purchases she wished to make for her culture. The first guinea would go towards a total revision of an educational system that still ignored the needs of women. With the second she would buy education for both men and women to increase people's tolerance for others and a deeper concern for justice. She offered her readers the third guinea with no restrictions as to its use.

As she had in *A Room of One's Own,* Virginia created imaginary conversations with both men and women who occupy various positions in society. In one section of the book, an all-male group offers Virginia a membership, which she turns down due to the group's historical disrespect for women. Instead, she creates the Outsider's Society for the "daughters of educated men," who will work to help support the men's group, but will elect no officers and hold no meetings of its own. A completely nonviolent group, it refuses to bear any type of arms. Virginia's point was that women did not need to follow in the footsteps of men. They could create their own society on their own terms.

The book received a mixed reception. Those who did not like it reacted intensely against it; those who liked it found it inspiring. One critic, Q.D. Leavis, who advocated the separation of art from politics, blasted it. He wrote that *A Room of One's Own* had been "annoying," but *Three Guineas* was "silly and ill-informed," containing "some dangerous assumptions, some preposterous claims, and some nasty attitudes." Regardless, the book remains a classic of feminist literature.

Virginia had to force herself to continue work on the biography of Roger Fry. It had begun as a labor of love, but in the meantime she had been struck by an idea for another novel and was eager to begin writing. The book started off titled *Pointz Hall* but would later be published as her final work, *Between the Acts*.

War loomed on the horizon and Virginia felt pressured to finish her works in progress. Trying to hurry through Fry's biography, she moved quickly through Roger's young adulthood, and then bogged down in the voluminous correspondence of his later years. She referred to the biography as a "barren nightmare," and found reading Vanessa's letters to Roger difficult. Not only did she read bitter comments about herself and Leonard, she also read Vanessa's remarks from 1915 about confining Virginia to a mental institution.

Although 1939 opened with unusually warm weather, Virginia worked indoors. Some smaller bits of her writing were published, including a short story titled "Lappin and Lapinova" in the American magazine, *Harper's Bazaar*. It was about a couple that had developed animal personas for one another, as had she and Leonard. She had also written an article about biographies, published by another U.S. magazine, the *Atlantic Monthly*.

As refugees from Europe began to flood England, the Woolfs offered help to various individuals, including one Jewish woman who brought with her family photographs that were later proved fake. Virginia was reminded that things were not always what they seemed. Vanessa urged her to begin her own autobiography, and the product was a brief memoir titled "A Sketch of the Past." As was the case with many of her projects, Virginia found the Fry biography exhausting in its final stages. All of her old doubts regarding her ability to write returned.

While Virginia's relationship with Vanessa remained strong, she was upset by the news that Angelica had begun an affair with Bunny Garnett, the man who had had a long-term affair with the girl's father, Duncan. When Bunny checked Angelica into a hospital with a kidney infection, rather than bring her home for care, Virginia wrote him an angry letter demanding that he bring her home. She regretted never having confronted him about his irresponsible attitudes in the past.

Virginia did her best to offer Leonard support when his publisher delayed publishing his book, *Barbarians at the Gate.* In the book Leonard attacked the weaknesses of capitalism almost as strongly as he did Nazism and fascism, which made his publisher nervous. When the book finally appeared later in the year, it received good notice. Curiously, the positive reception made Virginia resentful. She was also concerned about the coming war and growing old. She had promised Vanessa a copy of the Roger Fry biography to read by Christmas, but Christmas came and the book was still not done.

Leonard went ice skating on the final day of 1939, despite bitter cold. Storms caused the electricity to fail and snow covered the streets. However, Virginia again found inspiration in thoughts of Fry. In February 1940 she wrote a loving note to Vanessa:

> Sunday 4
> I've just been looking at my birthday present by daylight. It's a lovely picture—what a poet you are

Leonard and Virginia Woolf and Sally in 1939, the year World War II began in Europe. *(Photograph by Gisèle Freund.)*

in colour—one of these days I must write about you. And I do enjoy having a picture of my dear Quentin. What a pleasure your brats are to me—I long more and more for Julian, whose birthday it is today, and cant [sic] help just saying so, though I know you know it. My own darling I do think of you and him so much.

The picture to which she referred depicted Quentin reading, and it remained at Monk's House for decades.

Later in February, Virginia finally had a completed manuscript of the Fry biography to send to Roger's sister Margery. Margery suggested a few changes and Virginia agreed to make them. Leonard was critical of the book, saying Virginia had produced a boring work and had not remained faithful to the truth. The criticism seemed to weaken Virginia, and she immediately came down with the flu. A loving note from Vanessa lifted her spirits again, and she spent March correcting the manuscript.

In a speech she gave to the Workers Educational Association at Brighton that spring, she again stressed her belief that writing could not remain apolitical as it may have been in the past. Contemporary writers must insist that their literature react to the world. She hoped for a new literature that might represent a world with no class structure and no repression.

Angelica was now living with Bunny Garnett, her father's former lover. Despite her reservations about their relationship, Virginia continued her correspondence with her "Dearest Pixy." She entertained her niece with hu-

Roger Fry in 1932. Virginia's biography of him was published in 1940, six years after his death. *(Photograph by Ramsey and Muspratt, Cambridge.)*

morous descriptions of local events, including the establishment of fire escape routes and drills: "and old Miss Green aged 60 [let] herself down out of the Rectory window in shorts to show us how, when we're on fire." Her light tone masked her despair over the political situation. She and Leonard vowed to commit suicide by sitting in a running car in their closed garage if the Nazis reached England. The entire world seemed driven toward death.

As she thought about *Pointz Hall* and corrected proofs of *Roger Fry,* Virginia, along with the rest of England, waited for the threatened invasions of Britain and France. When Paris fell to the Germans, Leonard was miserable, thinking of all of his French friends who might have been killed or imprisoned. Virginia began carrying morphine in her pocket as a quick means of suicide.

Roger Fry appeared on July 25, 1940. Her friends and family felt the book restored their lost friend. More disinterested critics found it lacking. The book had a changing point of view, was poorly organized, and failed to be anything more than the traditional story of a life.

For once, Virginia had something more important than bad reviews to worry about. An invasion of England appeared imminent. The Woolfs did what they could to help refugees. When the first bombs fell in London, the Woolfs were outside. They lay face down under a tree, expecting to die. The serenity of Monk's House was shattered, and Virginia soon became used to hearing bombs and sirens. She wrote that observing a bomber in the air made her feel like a sardine watching a shark. Preparations for war on British soil proceeded at a furious rate, with men digging holes in the countryside in which to place large armaments. Virginia escaped into the writing of *Pointz Hall*.

There was no escape when, in September 1940, Vanessa's London studio and 52 Tavistock Square, Virginia's home, were bombed. When the Woolfs tried to get to their home, they were turned back by police, and a short time later another bomb inflicted so much destruction that they could no longer live in the house. They packed their printing press away to keep it safe.

The Woolfs returned to Monk's House, where Virginia continued to feel wounded by criticism of *Roger Fry*. In October the Woolfs and Vanessa visited their bombed out London houses. Large sections of walls, painted by Vanessa and Duncan, were exposed to the elements. Virginia wrote despairingly of the remaining wall that marked the studio where she had written so much. The loss of possessions did not bother her as much as the loss of her past. She was able to save her diaries and some dishes designed by Vanessa and Duncan.

The destruction seemed to spur her on as she revisited her family in "A Sketch of the Past," which focused on her parents and siblings. She also wrote a collection of essays titled *Anon* (short for "Anonymous," in honor of the many early women writers who did not sign their works) and an essay titled "The Reader" for a book on English literature. Virginia and Leonard visited Bunny and Angelica in the farmhouse they had rented near Vanessa's home in Charleston. They found Bunny disagreeable and Angelica's relationship with him "grotesque." Nothing could be done, however, and the Woolfs continued to socialize with the couple.

As another December approached, Virginia wrote that she could feel old age, with its hard edges, on her. "I am I," she wrote, adding that this was the "only justification for my writing & living." Although she did not record feeling the old demons of depression, she behaved strangely at times. Once, in a letter, she described the sheet of paper it was written on as being dirty and soiled. When the letter arrived, though, its recipient found it completely clean.

As 1941 began, Leonard noticed a change in Virginia's health. He asked for help from their friends. In January, she wrote of walking through London, once so lively a place, now observing its tattered neighborhoods with heaps of ashes and the skeletal remains of buildings. The public mood remained somber and many believed the Germans would obliterate them.

In February of 1941, Desmond MacCarthy (a former member of the Bloomsbury Group) attacked Virginia's essay, "The Leaning Tower." She had based it on the 1939 speech she delivered to the Workers Educational Association that called for writers to come out of their ivory towers and adopt a less idealistic attitude toward their cultures. MacCarthy wrote that Virginia could not possibly compare herself to workingmen, to which she retorted, "I never sat on top of a tower! Compare my wretched little £150 education with yours, with Lytton's, with Leonard's. . . . My tower was a mere toadstool." The fact MacCarthy missed her point about the quality of women's education greatly bothered her. Despite all she had done to argue for better conditions for women and to encourage a more imaginative approach to fiction, she often felt she had accomplished little. The public seemed just as rule-bound as ever, clinging to the past as it ignored a dark and threatening future.

Her latest novel, now renamed *Between the Acts,* neared conclusion. She wondered if she had managed to capture both the terror and the loveliness of life as she had hoped to do. She structured the novel as a linked series of scenes, with breaks indicated by white space on the page. As usual, Virginia remained more fascinated by form than plot. She made no attempt to connect the sections with transitions. As she had done before, Virginia asked readers to absorb a new approach to writing. The book focused on "private histories," the details of which formed the lives of characters that appear on earth for a brief time and then disappear.

Virginia Woolf in 1939. *(Photograph by Gisèle Freund.)*

In *Between the Acts,* Virginia combined many forms, including satire, drama, poetry, and fiction. One part of the book was an actual pageant, a satire on England's history, acted out by the novel's characters. Interspersed in the dialogue were fragments of characters' memories of their families, their histories, their pasts. The result was a dense, layered narrative that some readers would find depressing, others playfully ironic.

When Virginia mailed the manuscript to the publisher who had taken over Leonard's share of Hogarth Press, she noted in her cover letter that the book was "much too light and sketchy." Leonard had disagreed with her assessment, and her letter went on to ask the publisher's opinion on the matter. She added, "I feel fairly certain it would be a mistake from all points of view to publish it."

By March 1941, Virginia had descended into a dark mood. Even in the throes of her anxiety and depression, she continued her correspondence, clinging to the anchor of friendship that had always kept her in place. Nevertheless, she felt reality slipping away. Leonard confided to a visiting friend that he feared Virginia was in trouble.

On March 18, Leonard met Virginia as she was returning from a long walk. She was soaked through and muddy, and claimed to have fallen into a ditch. Leonard thought she might have tried to kill herself—later events seemed to confirm his suspicion. Over the next few days, Virginia wrote three suicide letters. In the first, written the day she had fallen into the water, she told Leonard that she felt sure madness approached, adding "You have given me the greatest possible happiness," but "I cant [sic] fight it any longer. I know that I am spoiling your life, that without me you could work. . . . If anybody could have saved me it would have been you."

Her second letter, dated five days later, was in response to a letter from Vanessa. Vanessa had ordered Virginia to rest and questioned how she and Leonard would handle an enemy invasion if Virginia became an invalid. This likely added to Virginia's concern. She wrote to Vanessa, thanking her for her concern and her love and saying, "But I feel that I have gone too far this time to come back again. I am certain now that I am going mad again . . . I am always hearing voices, and I know I shant [sic] get over it." She continued by praising Leonard, who she said had "been so astonishingly good, every day, always; I cant [sic] imagine that anyone could have done more for me than he has." That very day, she received a letter informing her that *Between the Acts* had been accepted for publication. She responded to this good news only with recommendations for improving the book. Her diary entry on March 24, the first she had written in over two weeks, was confused and incoherent.

On March 28, 1941, she wrote a third suicide note to her husband, reaffirming thoughts from the earlier letter and stressing, "that until this disease came on we were perfectly happy. It was all due to you . . . Everyone knows that." That same morning Leonard mailed Virginia's letter to her publisher, adding a postscript to the end noting that she stood on the brink of a breakdown. When he stepped outside to the garden, Virginia placed her letters on the mantelpiece in clear sight. Then she left the house by a back door.

A witness later described watching Virginia walk out the gate at the opposite end of the garden from where Leonard worked. She was dressed in her fur coat and her boots, and walked with the aid of a stick. When Leonard searched for her later, he found only her walking stick beside the Ouse River. A search for Virginia went on until some children playing at the river finally found her body nearly three weeks later, on April 18. She had loaded her pockets with stones to weigh herself down, and walked into the river to drown.

Chapter Eight

Legacy

Virginia Woolf's life remains as fascinating as her writings, both private and public. Scholars, students, and interested readers have studied her biography and her writings for decades. For a while after her death she was regarded as merely an artful intellectual. In the 1970s literary critics and intellectuals concerned with the equality of women resurrected her as a major writer. Her philosophy, political ideology, social convictions, and artistic ideas are combined in nine remarkable novels. Several of her works were at the forefront of what came to be called the modernist style of writing, a style that emphasized experimentalism in form and language.

Adrian Stephen, who had seen little of Virginia since 1930, died in 1948. One of his daughters would eventually contact Leonard, and they tried to make up for the gulf between their families. Vanessa Bell lived on until 1961, still married to Clive Bell but living happily with Duncan Grant. In her old age she withdrew into a private world that she allowed few people to share. The four grandchildren that followed Angelica's 1942 wedding to Bunny Garnett increased Vanessa's joy in her old age, although she never approved of the marriage.

Vanessa's children built careers around their famous aunt. Asked later to record a recollection of Virginia, Angelica wrote that her mother and aunt, "understood each other perfectly and were probably at their best in each other's company. They were bound together by the past, and perhaps also by the feeling that they were opposite in temperament and that what one lacked she could find only in the other." Angelica eventually separated from Bunny and became a writer herself, producing both a novel and a memoir. During the 1970s she lectured in the United States about her Aunt Virginia and the Bloomsbury Group.

Quentin Bell held many positions at various universities, including King's College and Oxford. He married Anne Olivier Popham in 1952, and she assisted him in editing Virginia's thirty notebooks of diary entries for publication between 1977 and 1984. Quentin Bell introduced the diaries as the last of her writing that the public would enjoy, and believed they should be included among her major works. He felt these writings were themselves masterpieces, works just as important as Virginia's novels. She had used her diaries as working writers should, to reflect on the world around her, and to speculate how she might use that reflection in her art.

At Leonard Woolf's request, in 1972, Quentin produced the most well-known biography of his famous

Leonard Woolf, pictured here with Virginia's diary, lived until 1969. *(Photograph by Gisèle Freund.)*

aunt. Several critics attacked the biography for including so little information about Virginia Woolf's writings. Later critics agreed that this biography is essential reading for those who desire details of Virginia's life, but that it must be supplemented by material that focuses specifically on her writing. With Angelica, Quentin became an executor of his aunt's literary estate after Leonard's death.

Leonard Woolf lived another twenty-eight years. After Virginia's body was found, he had been the one to identify her, after which he had suffered through an inquest, experiences that he found tortuous. Virginia had asked to be cremated, and when he explained to Vanessa that he planned to spread Virginia's ashes in the garden at Monk's House, under a huge elm tree that the couple had named Virginia, he broke down and sobbed. He placed a sculpture of Virginia's head close to the tree and posted as her epitaph the closing words of *The Waves:* "Against you I will fling myself, unvanquished and unyielding, O Death!"

Leonard also wrote a five-volume autobiography in the 1950s. Over the years, he rebutted every attack on Virginia's writing and sorted carefully through all of her papers. In the margin of her final suicide note, Virginia had written "Will you destroy all my papers," but Leonard destroyed none of them.

Leonard Woolf issued collections of Virginia's essays as well as selected correspondence with Lytton Strachey, but sentiment against the Bloomsbury Group in the 1950s convinced him not to publish additional correspondence at that time. As no library in England wanted Virginia's papers, he sent most of them to the New York Public Library. In America, scholars eagerly awaited Leonard's gift, producing volumes upon volumes of research related to Virginia Woolf. Professional academic societies and journals sprung up in her name, and studying her work became enormously popular.

This bust of Virginia Woolf stands in the garden at Monk's House.

Between 1975 and 1980, nearly four thousand of Woolf's letters were collected and published in six volumes by the Hogarth Press in England. They would later be published in the United States.

Leonard Woolf died at age eighty-eight, on August 14, 1969. As he had done for Virginia, his friends scattered his ashes beneath the elm tree next to hers, the one that they had named Leonard. A bust of Leonard was placed on the wall where he had installed a similar one of Virginia. Family and friends felt they both belonged in the garden that they had so loved, gazing into the countryside where they had spent so many years working, thinking, and loving together.

Timeline

1882	Adeline Virginia Stephen is born to Julia Duckworth and Leslie Stephen on January 25.
1890	Writes and edits family newspaper titled *Hyde Park Gate News.*
1895	Death of mother; Virginia has first mental breakdown.
1899	Thoby Stephen enters Trinity College; Virginia meets Lytton Strachey, Leonard Woolf, and Clive Bell—members of the future Bloomsbury Group.
1902	Leslie Stephen receives knighthood.
1904	Death of father; Virginia has second mental breakdown; moves to 46 Gordon Square with sister Vanessa and brother Adrian; publishes first review, anonymously.
1905	Stephen children travel to Greece.
1906	Death of Thoby Stephen.
1907	Marriage of Vanessa to Clive Bell; Virginia begins *Melymbrosia,* later her first novel, renamed *Voyage Out.*
1910	Meets Roger Fry, organizer of the first postimpressionist exhibit at Grafton Galleries.
1912	Marries Leonard Woolf; Leonard helps Fry with second postimpressionist exhibit.
1913	First novel, *Voyage Out,* completed; third mental breakdown.
1914	A year of recovery.
1915	*Voyage Out* published; begins keeping a diary in earnest.
1917	Regular contributor to *Times Literary Supplement;* initiation of Hogarth Press with *Two Stories.*

1918 Considers part of Joyce's *Ulysses* manuscript for publication by Hogarth.

1919 Publishes *Night and Day*—public discussion of "modern fiction."

1920 Writes short stories including "Kew Gardens."

1922 Publishes the novel *Jacob's Room;* meets Vita Sackville-West.

1924 Lecturers on "modern fiction"; Hogarth publishes "Mr. Bennet and Mrs. Brown."

1925 Publishes *Mrs. Dalloway;* publishes first essay collection, *The Common Reader.*

1926 Diary entry idea for "semi-mystic profound life of a woman": basis for *The Waves.*

1927 Publishes *To the Lighthouse;* lectures at Oxford on "Poetry, Fiction and the Future."

1928 Publishes *Orlando,* dedicated to Vita Sackville-West; reading of papers that later become *A Room of One's Own.*

1929 Publishes *A Room of One's Own.*

1930 Completes first draft and begins second draft of *The Moths,* which later becomes *The Waves.*

1931 Publishes *The Waves.*

1932 Publishes *The Common Reader, Second Series;* Lytton Strachey dies.

1936 Tormented completion of *The Years.*

1937 Publishes eighth novel, *The Years;* Julian Bell killed in Spanish Civil War.

1938 Publishes feminist novel, *Three Guineas;* begins work on new novel titled *Pointz Hall,* which later becomes her final novel, *Between the Acts.*

1939 Begins memoir, "A Sketch of the Past."

1940 Completes biography, *Roger Fry.*

1941 Completes *Between the Acts* in February; commits suicide on March 28.

Sources

CHAPTER ONE: Adeline Virginia Stephen

p. 11, "looking-glasses possessing…" Virginia Woolf, *A Room of One's Own* (New York: Harcout, Brace and Co., 1981), 32.

p. 11, "I fancy sometimes…" Virginia Woolf, *The Diary of Virginia Woolf,* vol. 3., ed. Anne Olivier Bell (New York: Harcourt, Brace and Co., 1982), 201.

p. 12, "My cheeks had burned" Woolf, *A Room of One's Own,* 33.

p. 12, "the first major achievement…" Sandra M. Gilbert and Susan Gubar, eds., "Virginia Woolf: 1882-1941," *The Norton Anthology of Literature by Women: The Traditions in English,* 2nd ed. (New York: W.W. Norton & Co., 1996), 1317.

p. 18, "explored…private parts" Panthea Reid, *Art and Affection:A Life of Virginia Woolf* (Oxford: Oxford University Press, 1996), 24.

p. 20, "serene and practical…wild and impish" George Spater and Ian Parsons, *A Marriage of True Minds: An Intimate Portrait of Leonard and Virginia Woolf* (New York: Harcourt, Brace, Jovanovich, 1977), 10.

p. 22, "hardworking, ambitious…" Reid, *Art and Affection,* 28.

p. 22, "nine in years…" Ibid., 34.

p. 23, "Hold yourself straight…" Ibid., 40.

p. 23, "everything had come to an end" Mark Hussey, *Virginia Woolf: A-Z* (Oxford: Oxford University Press, 1995), 268.

p. 23, "She grew whiter…" Ibid., 77.

p. 24, "she must do less lessons..." Ibid., 44.

p. 24, "musical" Ibid., 77.

CHAPTER TWO: The Bloomsbury Group

p. 30, "at the back of the eye...one's breath away." Spater and Parsons, *A Marriage of True Minds,* 25.

p. 31, "Everyone has forgotten me...we shall be ruined" Ibid.

p. 32, "I think Providence..." Quentin Bell, *Virginia Woolf: A Biography,* vol. 1 (London: Hogarth Press, 1990), 79.

p. 39, "filled with wonder" Quentin Bell, vol. 1, 98.

p. 39, "piling stone upon stone..." Ibid.

p. 39, "something miraculous..." Ibid.

p. 40, "the young men..." Spater and Parsons, *A Marriage of True Minds,* 39.

p. 42, "in the midst of nurses..." Ibid., 109.

p. 44, "We were the most incompatible..." Ibid., 40.

p. 44, "Adrian stalked off..." Ibid.

p. 45, "in a person I cared for..." Clive Bell, *Old Friends: Personal Recollections* (London: Chatto & Windus, 1956), 93.

p. 46, "attain a different..." Reid, *Art and Affection,* 94.

p. 46, "shivering fragments" Ibid.

p. 47, "do not know..." Ibid., 101.

CHAPTER THREE: Mrs. Leonard Woolf

p. 52, "I could not write . . ." Quentin Bell, *Virginia Woolf,* 176.

p. 54, "You're the only . . ." Ibid., 182.

p. 54, "God the happiness . . ." Ibid., 184-85.

p. 54, "in a fog" Ibid.

p. 55, "some feeling which..." Ibid.

p. 55, "I'm going to marry . . .the best part of me." Ibid., vol 2, 2.

p. 56, "the mind and heart . . ." Spater and Parsons, *A Marriage of True Minds,* 81.

p. 56, "appallingly stupid..." Ibid., 67.

p. 62, "few things at ..." Virginia Woolf, *The Voyage Out* (San Diego: Harvest/Harcourt Brace Jovanovich, 1948), 164.

p. 62, "if I were a woman..." Ibid., 215.
p. 64, "written by a woman..." Hussey, *Virginia Woolf,* 339.
p. 64, "never was a book..." Ibid., 339.

CHAPTER FOUR: The Writing Life

p. 68, "seems to lull...wonderfully harmonious." Clive Bell, *Old Friends,* 32.
p. 71, "perfect" Reid, *Art and Affection,* 199.
p. 72, "an American of the highest..." Spater and Parsons, *A Marriage of True Minds,* 102.
p. 78, "write a novel about Silence..." Hussey, *Virginia Woolf,* 188.
p. 78, "so exciting..." Spater and Parsons, *A Marriage of True Minds,* 94.
p. 81, "change and develop..." Reid, *Art and Affection,* 256.
p. 81, "it does not..." Spater and Parsons, *A Marriage of True Minds,* 97.
p. 81, "reproachfully post-impressionist" Reid, *Art and Affection,* 258.
p. 81, "prose-poem" Spater and Parsons, *A Marriage of True Minds,* 94.
p. 83, "At that one feels...certain melancholy" Virginia Woolf, *The Diary of Virginia Woolf,* vol. 2, ed. Anne Olivier Bell (New York: Harcourt, Brace and Company, 1978), 226-27.

CHAPTER FIVE: "A Room of One's Own"

p. 84, "Never settle..." Woolf, *The Diary,* vol. 2, 259.
p. 85, "Youth is a matter of..." Ibid., 281-82.
p. 86, "last lap of Mrs. D...." Ibid., 312.
p. 90, "We walk home from..." Ibid., 291.
p. 94, "a psychological poem" Hussey, *Virginia Woolf,* 311.
p. 94, "very beautiful..." Ibid.
p. 95, "an old and valued..." Ibid., 197.
p. 95, "a high brow lark." Hussey, *Virginia Woolf,* 204.
p. 95, "a poetic masterpiece." Ibid.

p. 96, "vaults in some…" Ibid., 201.

p. 97, "But she lives…" Virginia Woolf, *A Room of One's Own,* 113.

p. 97, "starved but valiant…" Woolf, *The Diary,* vol. 3, 200.

p. 97, "drink wine & have a room…" Ibid.

p. 97, "grown heavy…" Ibid., 209.

p. 97, "haunted" Ibid., 218.

p. 98, "transitory, flying, diaphanous…" Ibid.

p. 98, "One ought perhaps…" Ibid., 219.

CHAPTER SIX: The Best and the Worst

p. 99, "like a fly on gummed …" Woolf, *The Diary,* vol. 3, 285.

p. 100, "the moth [was] shaking…" Ibid., 287.

p. 100, "children are nothing" Ibid., 298.

p. 100, "see the last lap…" Ibid., 301.

p. 100, "angel of the house" Virginia Woolf, "Professions for Women," *Women and Writing,* ed. Michele Barrett (San Diego: Harcourt Brace & Co., 1979), 59.

p. 102, "series of dramatic soliloquies" Woolf, *The Diary,* vol. 3, 312.

p. 104, "art, architecture…" Ibid., 168.

p. 105, "run gaily and swiftly…" Ibid., 172.

p. 105, "the batting, the laughter…" Virginia Woolf, *The Diary of Virginia Woolf,* vol. 4, ed. Anne Olivier Bell (New York: Harcourt, Brace and Company, 1982), 211.

p. 107, "strike the match…the right tone of voice." Ibid.

p. 107, "I think the poverty…" Ibid., 242.

CHAPTER SEVEN: New Wars

p. 114, "daughters of educated men" Hussey, *Virginia Woolf,* 288.

p. 114, "annoying…nasty attitudes." Ibid., 295.

p. 115, "barren nightmare" Reid, *Art and Affection,* 400.

p. 116, "Sunday 4,…" Virginia Woolf, *The Letters of Virginia Woolf,* vol. 6: 1936-1941, eds. Nigel Nicolson and Joanne Trautmann (New York: Harcourt, Brace, Jovanovich, 1980), 381.

p. 119, "Dearest Pixy" Ibid., 405.

p. 119, "and old Miss Green..." Ibid.

p. 121, "grotesque" Reid, *Art and Affection,* 432.

p. 121, "I am I..." Ibid., 434.

p. 122, "I never sat..." Ibid., 437.

p. 122, "private histories" Hussey, *Virginia Woolf,* 26.

p. 124, "much too light and sketchy" Woolf, *The Letters* vol. 6, 482.

p. 124, "I feel fairly certain..." Ibid.

p. 124, "You have given me..." Ibid., 481.

p. 125, "But I feel..." Ibid., 485.

p. 125, "that until this disease..." Ibid., 487.

CHAPTER EIGHT: Legacy

p. 128, "understood each other..." Joan Russell Noble, ed., *Recollections of Virginia Woolf by her Contemporaries* (London: Peter Owen, 1972), 87-88.

p. 130, "Against you I will fling myself..." Virginia Woolf, *The Waves* (New York: Harcourt Brace & World, 1959), 297.

p. 130, "Will you destroy all my papers," Woolf, *The Letters,* vol. 6, xi.

Bibliography

Bell, Clive. *Old Friends: Personal Recollections.* London: Chatto & Windus, 1956.

Bell, Quentin. *Virginia Woolf: A Biography.* London: Hogarth Press, 1990.

Bennett, Joan. *Virginia Woolf: Her Art as a Novelist.* Cambridge: Cambridge University Press, 1964.

Brewster, Dorothy. *Virginia Woolf.* New York: New York University Press, 1962.

Gilbert, Sandra M., and Susan Gubar, eds. "Virginia Woolf: 1882-1941." *The Norton Anthology of Literature by Women: The Traditions in English.* 2nd ed. New York: W.W. Norton & Co., 1996.

Guiget, Jean. *Virginia Woolf and Her Works.* New York: Harcourt Brace & World, 1962.

———. Preface. *Contemporary Writers.* New York: Harcourt Brace & World, 1965.

Hussey, Mark. *Virginia Woolf: A-Z.* Oxford: Oxford University Press, 1995.

Noble, Joan Russell, ed. *Recollections of Virginia Woolf.* London: Peter Owen, 1972.

Paul, Janis. *The Victorian Heritage of Virginia Woolf; The External World in her Novels.* Norman, OK: Pilgrim Books, 1987.

Reid, Panthea. *Art and Affection: A Life of Virginia Woolf.* Oxford: Oxford University Press, 1996.

Spater, George and Ian Parsons. *A Marriage of True Minds: An Intimate Portrait of Leonard and Virginia Woolf.* New York: Harcourt, Brace, Jovanovich, 1977.

Warner, Eric. *Virginia Woolf: The Waves.* Cambridge: Cambridge University Press, 1987.

Woolf, Virginia. *A Room of One's Own.* 1929. Reprint, New York: Harcourt, Brace, Jovanovich, 1957.

————. *Contemporary Writers.* New York: Harcourt Brace & World, 1965.

————. *The Diary of Virginia Woolf.* Vol. 1. Edited by Anne Olivier Bell. New York: Harcourt, Brace and Company, 1977.

————. *The Diary of Virginia Woolf.* Vol. 2. Edited by Anne Olivier Bell. New York: Harcourt, Brace and Company, 1978.

————. *The Diary of Virginia Woolf.* Vol. 3. Edited by Anne Olivier Bell. New York: Harcourt, Brace and Company, 1982.

————. *The Diary of Virginia Woolf.* Vol. 4. Edited by Anne Olivier Bell. New York: Harcourt, Brace and Company, 1982.

————. *The Letters of Virginia Woolf.* Vol. 6: 1936-1941. Edited by Nigel Nicolson and Joanne Trautmann. New York: Harcourt, Brace, Jovanovich, 1980.

————. *Mrs. Dalloway.* New York: Harcourt Brace & World, 1925.

————. *The Voyage Out.* 1920. Reprint, San Diego: Harvest/Harcourt, Brace, Jovanovich, 1948.

————. *The Waves.* New York: Harcourt Brace & World, 1959.

————. "Professions for Women." *Women and Writing.* Edited by Michele Barrett. San Diego: Harcourt Brace & Co., 1979.

Index